THE TAPPAN ZEE BRIDGE AND THE

FORGING OF THE ROCKLAND SUBURB

JERRY

Thanks for your contributions
to our oral history project
of the opening

D. Parrot

2 MARCH 2010

THE

TAPPAN ZEE

BRIDGE

AND

THE FORGING

OF THE

ROCKLAND SUBURB

ROGER PANETTA

The Historical Society of Rockland County

THE HISTORICAL SOCIETY OF ROCKLAND COUNTY

20 Zukor Road, New City, NY 10956

Printed in the United States of America

First Edition 2010

Library of Congress Cataloging-in-Publication Data

Panetta, Roger G., 1939–

    The Tappan Zee Bridge and the forging of the Rockland suburb / by Roger Panetta.

      p.   cm.

ISBN-13: 978-0-911183-15-3 (pbk.)

ISBN-10: 0-911183-15-9 (pbk.)

1. Tappan Zee Bridge (N.Y.) 2. Suburbs—New York (State)—Rockland County—History. I. Title.

TG25.N538P36   2009

388.1′320974728—dc22

2009045456

Half title image: *Piermont Moon*. Courtesy Estate of Charles W. Norton Jr.
Frontispiece: Aerial photograph, looking east. HRSC Collection
Rockland County map by Sharon M. Okada

Designed by Lisa Hamm

Publication of *The Tappan Zee Bridge and the Forging of the Rockland Suburb* was supported by a Preserve America grant from the National Park Service, initiated by Rockland County Executive C. Scott Vanderhoef.

The material in this book is based upon work assisted by a grant from the Department of the Interior, National Park Service. Any opinions, findings, and conclusions or recommendations expressed in this material are those of the author and do not necessarily reflect the views of the Department of the Interior.

Dr. Thomas F. X. Casey
1935–2009

Senior Historian and Former President
The Historical Society of Rockland County
Historian of the County of Rockland

CONTENTS

FOREWORD

I
T WAS inevitable that in the mid-twentieth century Rockland County, the simple, rustic area so very close to New York City, would find connection to the greater world, especially in the urban migration following World War II. That the road to the future arrived at Nyack with a Hudson River highway crossing from Tarrytown was more than convenience. It was fate. The opening of the Tappan Zee Bridge on December 15, 1955 began a union between a rural farming/industrial community and the relatively cosmopolitan suitor who would come to live here. The first child of that match was the fledgling suburb, its roots now grown into a family tree of added diversity, community success and failure, models of reasonable growth and poor planning, hope, opportunity, and direction, as well as concern for what's ahead.

Even as Washington and Albany contemplate whether to continue and perhaps deepen Rockland's connections to other peoples and other areas with a new crossing from Nyack, there is much history to be told about the growth of the county encouraged by the bridge. As author Roger Panetta writes in his summation of *The Tappan Zee Bridge and the Forging of the Rockland Suburb*, this is the "story of modern America."

With the financial decision in the early 1950s to place a major revenue-producing river crossing at Nyack rather than end the thruway at Suffern, where it was to connect with Bergen County roads to New York City, the thruway Authority put Rockland within reach of the city and Westchester County, transforming a sparsely populated, countrified community into a destination for, as Panetta writes, "a great migration of peoples of many races, different classes, various religions, and many points of origin; some came from nearby cities and some from distant places . . . in search of the postwar American Dream of the single-family home with its promise of community and harmony."

It is Professor Panetta's thesis that "While at times we lament the excesses of sprawl, we need to recognize the aspirations of all who crossed the bridge. This monumental structure bore promises of hope and renewal." Ah, that is the optimistic side of a debate among Rocklanders that began as soon as the bridge was proposed, continues to this day, and is increasing, given plans for the new crossing.

The pessimistic side of Rockland as a suburb is that while the marriage of outside suitor and local maiden offered fertility for the aspirations of thousands who might not otherwise have had opportunity, the consequence of the large family that has taken root in the county is far-reaching suburban sprawl that cannot be ignored. That added housing and shopping density will continue to arrive at greater cost in property taxes, more schools, bigger government, new infrastructure, and environmental stress. And even as a new crossing at the Tappan Zee is proposed, though no one knows where the money will come from, so too, some argue, the expense of maintaining and renewing the "graying suburb" spawned a half century ago will prove insurmountable.

The major and growing criticism of the suburb anywhere is the inherent anonymity in which neighbors may live for years on the same development street without knowing each other's names. Vehicles are necessary to go everywhere—shopping, to school, to work, to see friends. Contrast that existence to small, pre–Tappan Zee Bridge Rockland, where towns and villages provided walkable shopping areas and were home to long-standing families who knew other long-standing families. In the same fashion, thousands of suburban arrivals came from old, well-established New York City neighborhoods in which blocks of people interacted with one another.

The early suburb in Rockland continued some of this rural/urban closeness through energized PTAs, service organizations, civic associations, and block parties, but resale, larger developments, longer commuting time, and two-wage-earner families have pushed us all into busy lives and consequent anonymity amid a large population.

Yet such pessimism is not in the professor's script. His scholarly look at prewar Rockland, with its farms and industry, county fairs, utopian communities, and famous artists, writers, and thespians, sets the stage for the magnetism of the smallest county geographically in New York State, outside Gotham. Panetta describes the summer bungalows that introduced families to Rockland; people remembered the bucolic relief from the hot city, and so, when the Tappan Zee Bridge and the Palisades Interstate Parkway opened commuting routes, they moved.

He also details the engineering concerns of the bridge crossing at such a wide point in the Hudson River, where bedrock is so deep that the superstructure must float on caissons. These devices, made possible by World War II technology, became a metaphor for the crossing itself and the possibility it afforded urbanites for a new and better existence after the war.

The professor gives us a panoramic view of the American suburb that is Rockland, from the time just after the bridge opened through the early growth difficulties, later sprawl, and the building of a highly controversial shopping center, the Palisades Center Mall, a symbol to some of the consequences of poor suburban planning. Finally, Panetta details the plans for and debate about a second coming of the road to suburbia, concluding, "The building of the bridge was a decisive moment in Rockland's history. And in this new connection, breaching the water boundary, overcoming the obstacles of nature, we find the origins of modern Rockland County." It is a Rockland sure to be further defined by the growth and other changes prompted by both its suburban legacy and a new, bigger crossing at the Tappan Zee.

Arthur H. Gunther III
Blauvelt, New York

ACKNOWLEDGMENTS

EVERY FALL as I looked out at the Hudson through my west window, at Marymont College in Tarrytown, into the clear night, I was often startled by the lights of the Tappan Zee Bridge and their shimmering reflection on the river. These evening light shows continued in the months ahead and became even more vivid in the crisp, cold nights of winter. Gradually the individual experiences began to have a deeper collective impact beyond my momentary aesthetic appreciation.

I began to see the bridge as a kind of intellectual Trojan horse, hiding within itself an important piece of history of the Hudson River. What new possibilities did it suggest for research and writing? When I looked west every evening, what did I see? Or more important, what did I *not* see? In spite of these annual epiphanies, my interest in the bridge long lay dormant, appearing only as a footnote in my ramblings about the Hudson and the region.

In a chance meeting with Gretchen Weerheim, Curator of Education at The Historical Society of Rockland County, my curiosity about the Tappan Zee found a sympathetic ear. Planning meetings we had with Executive Director Erin L. Martin, former Society President Thomas F. X. Casey, and Curator Jessica Kuhnen led to the organization of the Tappan Zee Bridge Project and an invitation for me to direct this undertaking.

The project, inspired by the 2009 Hudson-Fulton-Champlain Quadricentennial, included four components: an oral history outreach, guided by Dr. Travis Jackson; an exhibition, "The Tappan Zee Bridge: Transforming Rockland County," curated by Jessica Kuhnen; an educational DVD for schools, developed by Gretchen Weerheim; and finally this book, which serves as a capstone history for the project. My writing benefited greatly from numerous conversations with colleagues at the Society—especially the research support from Jessica Kuhnen in locating documents and images from the collection. Craig H. Long's exhaustive three volumes of newspaper clippings on the Tappan Zee Bridge were especially helpful.

As the project's scope grew and the size of its budget increased, Erin Martin worked tirelessly to integrate the distinct pieces, keep them moving forward, and secure a Preserve America grant to sustain our work. A countywide committee with representatives from local historical societies and government helped us clarify our goals and develop close links to Rockland's communities. County Tourism Director Heather Duke, Jason Rielly from the County Executive's office, and David Banks from the National Park Service were most helpful.

The New York State Thruway Authority reached into its archives and generously provided source materials and a number of vivid photographs, many of which are included in this text. Special appreciation goes to their staff, especially Polly Gurnett, Records Access Officer, for their efforts in locating and sharing this material with us.

Arthur H. Gunther III drew on his long experience as a journalist and chronicler of Rockland's recent history to contribute the foreword and help me avoid the missteps of the outsider.

Marianne B. Leese closely read several versions of the text and provided invaluable editorial assistance, and recommended additional sources for my research. I am very grateful for her patience and the generous contribution of her time.

Leslie Kriesel and Lisa Hamm provided respectively the copyediting and design, and general advice that enhanced the quality of this book. It is a pleasure to continue to work with these two professionals.

My wife, Eileen Panetta, provided a testing ground for much of my thinking about the Tappan Zee Bridge and joined in many discussions during the preparation of this manuscript. Crossing the bridge is for both of us no longer just a stepping-stone to somewhere else.

THE TAPPAN ZEE BRIDGE AND THE

FORGING OF THE ROCKLAND SUBURB

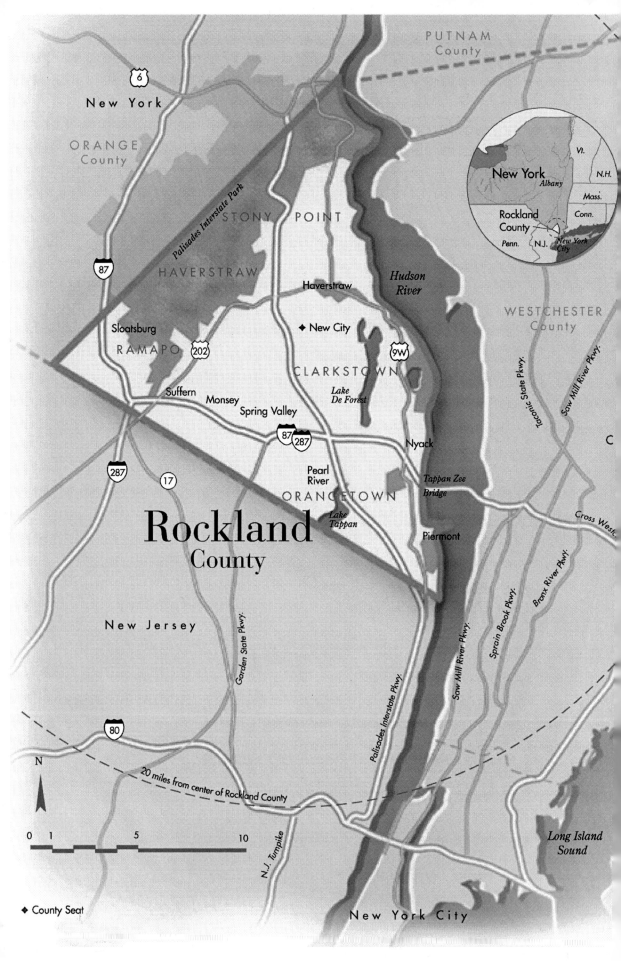

PUTNAM
County

6
New York

ORANGE
County

Palisades Interstate Park

STONY POINT

HAVERSTRAW

87

Haverstraw

Hudson
River

Sloatsburg

RAMAPO

202

♦ New City

9W

WESTCHESTER
County

Suffern

Monsey

Spring Valley

CLARKSTOWN

Lake
De Forest

87 287

Nyack

287

17

Pearl
River

ORANGETOWN

Tappan Zee
Bridge

Rockland
County

Lake
Tappan

Piermont

Cross West.

Taconic State Pkwy.

Saw Mill River Pkwy.

C

New Jersey

Garden State Pkwy.

Palisades Interstate Pkwy.

Saw Mill River Pkwy.

Sprain Brook Pkwy.

Bronx River Pkwy.

80

N

20 miles from center of Rockland County

Long Island
Sound

0 1   5   10

N.J. Turnpike

New York City

New York

Albany

Rockland
County

Penn.

N.J.

New York
City

Vt.

N.H.

Mass.

Conn.

♦ County Seat

A MERICANS LOVE bridges. We are fascinated by their engineering, their challenge to the obstacles of nature, and the courage and ingenuity of their builders. Some structures, like the Brooklyn Bridge, have become historic American icons celebrated and studied by many. Focus on the bridges themselves can at times obscure or overlook the impact these great structures have on the landscape and communities they connect.

Bridges are also political and cultural works, and the debates and plans about their shape, size, and location are an important part of the story. Because these structures seem so permanent and durable, their histories take on the quality of the inevitable. But a closer look at the history of the Tappan Zee Bridge tells us otherwise.

This book will examine the role of the Tappan Zee Bridge in the forging of the Rockland County suburb. From its initial planning through its construction to the current visions for rebuilding, the bridge has radically transformed a rural sanctuary into a dynamic suburb.

GEOGRAPHY

Henry Hudson sailed up the Hudson River in the quest for the Northwest Passage and, on September 14, 1609, entered a wide natural sea—a great, open ellipse measuring three miles at its widest point and ten miles long. He was elated, believing that he had found the long-sought water route across the continent, but after eleven days moving north, he reached the shallower waters near Albany and realized his mistake. He was now in a river, a freshwater source.

This sea within the river that Hudson explored was named the Tappan after the local native Lenape community and *Zee* from the Dutch word for sea. A second expanse of water farther north—Haverstraw Bay—mirrors the Tappan Zee and completes the water boundary of eastern Rockland County. The names Tappan, Haverstraw, and Nyack recall the native history of the area—the first people to navigate the great river crossing in their dugout canoes.

The Hudson River cut through the valley, creating an eastern and a western shore—a water barrier that seemed destined to keep two worlds separate and unreconciled. In its earliest history, the river had turned westward and inland to the southwest, away from the great ocean. When the ancient river breached the ridge and pushed directly southward, it changed the history of the Tappan Zee and Rockland. The power of geography to shape history is clearly evident in the distinctive stories of Rockland and Westchester counties. Their locations would over time determine residents' access to the great metropolis at the mouth of the river. The natural boundary of the Hudson insulated Rockland from the first wave of nineteenth-century suburbanization that transformed Westchester and allowed the western shore to retain its rural character and farm culture.

Rockland's eastern water boundary forms part of the triangle that came to mark the county's lines. Dutch settlements began in 1675 when Harmansen Dowesen Tallman arrived in Nyack. As early as 1666, Balthazar De Harte had acquired the Haverstraw riverfront; other speculative purchases followed, instigated by the river connection to New Amsterdam. But conflicts with native peoples kept the area unsettled into the latter part of the seventeenth century. The role of the Hudson in the early history of Rockland was formative.[1]

During the colonial period, many stores were located at river landings. Farm products, including vegetables, meat, butter, and eggs, were exchanged for tea, coffee, sugar, and other imported and manufactured goods. Milled flour would be shipped to New York City by wagon or sloop. Some hardy traders made their way there on foot. Soon sloops were making regular trips to New York. Rockland's economic and commercial life in the eighteenth century was becoming intertwined with the river and the city.

TRANSPORTATION

On February 23, 1789, Orange County was divided and the southern region was designated Rockland County, a comment on the character of the landscape.

The Kings Highway connected the early colonial settlements along the Hudson River, which extended from Tappan to Haverstraw and Stony Point, pushing on to Albany. After the Revolution, a system of roads was developed. Old trails and native paths were widened and established the routes for later concrete and asphalt highways. Route 17, one of the oldest post roads to Albany, served as a winter alternative to the frozen Hudson. Suffern became a hub, its roads extending north and west into New York State and south and east into New Jersey and Connecticut. In 1816 a bill to construct a turnpike between Nyack and Suffern introduced in the State Assembly did not pass, but by the 1830s the Nyack Turnpike provided a straight route across the county; Route 59 is its modern reincarnation. The exchange of bricks and wood required a road between Suffern and Haverstraw, the forerunner of Route 202. Many of these roads linked Rockland to the Hudson and reinforced the importance of the river towns of Nyack and Haverstraw. Through the nineteenth century, road building continued, and in 1894 Rockland legislated a county road system. By the end of the century, of the seventy-two miles of roads, more than half were still dirt and only a third macadamized.[2]

Railroads improved the movement of goods and people. In May 1841, the New York and Erie began service between Piermont and Spring Valley, extending to Goshen by September 1841. Other new lines, such as the Hackensack & New York in 1872, linked to New York City via ferries, while the Erie created new business opportunities for Rocklanders. The West Shore Railroad hugged the Hudson as it traveled north to south. By century's end, most Rockland communities were linked by a jerry-built rail system. This new network served as a catalyst for nineteenth-century industrial development and created an economy that was increasingly diverse and deeply engaged in serving the New York City market.

INDUSTRY

Home manufacturing moved beyond subsistence as the expanding transportation connections at Haverstraw, Nyack, Suffern, and Tappan pushed businessmen and farmers beyond the goal of self-sufficiency to the expectation of profit. Sawmills and gristmills tapped the natural resource of water power, and soon other businesses recognized in the gifts of nature new opportunities. Rocks and stones, so detested by farmers, yielded red and gray sandstone quarries at Nyack: thirty-nine quarries between Upper Nyack and Grand View employed hundreds of workers. Docks extended far out into the Hudson to load barges with the free-stone bound for New York City.

Crushed stone from the traprock industry, located in the ridges and other rock outcrops in the Hudson River Valley, especially the Palisades, furnished material for New York City's seawalls, docks, and railroads, and in the twentieth century for major regional highways. Traprock provided the hard bulk in composite materials that were bonded together in concrete and macadam. Quarries were developed in Clarkstown, Upper Nyack, Tomkins Cove, and Haverstraw.[3]

Brick making, which flourished in the nineteenth century, had colonial roots in the Hudson Valley and began in Rockland in the 1770s. Haverstraw became the brick-making capital of the United States, extending from the Short Clove to the Stony Point Battlefield. The demand for bricks in an expanding New York City was insatiable, and after the Great Fires of 1835 and 1845, fire resistance regulations meant brick walls and more business for Rockland's brick manufacturers.[4] It was a sellers' market, but pricing was increasingly unpredictable. Forty brick-yards produced more than three hundred million bricks annually and employed hundreds of workers. African Americans were favored—"more thrifty and cause less trouble."[5] The industry was concentrated in Rockland, peaked in 1890, and declined in the early twentieth century. Most of the bricks were shipped by barge to New York City.

Clay was increasingly dredged from the river, and the biggest clay pit, now the Haverstraw Marina, served as the site for the construction of the Tappan Zee Bridge caissons, which were floated down the Hudson to the bridge construction site.[6] The aggressive extraction of clay, from Bowline Point lands extending alongside the river in Haverstraw, created an artificial ridge with houses perched above the pits. Not surprisingly, this kind of dangerous excavating precipitated the great landslide of 1906, which destroyed lives, property, and businesses in Haverstraw.[7] Legal battles and injunctions could not restrain the brick makers, and on January 8, 1906,

> like the movement of a distant earthquake . . . the buildings began to quiver. In a second the loosened sections of the bank gathered momentum and then, with a terrific roar, it began to move toward the chasm with a rapidity of lightning while the houses, with a frightening grinding sound, were crushed like fragile glass vases.[8]

Houses and streets darkened, and 19 lives were lost in one of the earliest environmental disasters in the county. The battle between development and profit

(top and bottom) Haverstraw landslide, 1906 *HSRC Collection*

and community health and safety was won by the brick makers, who recovered $200,000 worth of clay from the slide.[9]

Transportation initially depended on sloops and schooners. In the nineteenth century, steam-powered tugs hauled brick barges to New York City in groups called "tows." The downriver location of Rockland gave it a decided edge over more northern competitors. This symbiotic relationship between county and city is fundamental to understanding Rockland's economic dependence on New York

The large icehouse at Rockland Lake, circa 1915 *HSRC Collection*

Cutting ice at Rockland Lake, circa 1910 *HSRC Collection*

Workers at Peck Brickyard, circa 1902 *HSRC Collection*

and the Hudson River. The shadow of New York City reached as far north as the Tappan Zee.

The ice industry mimicked brick making by using the river to transport a Rockland commodity to the New York market. The regional Hudson Valley ice industry, consisting of more than a hundred businesses located along the river as far north as Albany, was concentrated in the south at Rockland Lake, where at its peak more than a thousand men harvested ice for the Knickerbocker Ice Company. Rockland businessman Moses Leonard took samples of Rockland ice to New York and won many customers.[10] Ice cut at the lake was stored in icehouses and eventually conveyed by cable car to the river landing, then towed by sloop and steamboat on large barges to Yonkers, Manhattan, and Brooklyn. Other Rockland lakes were tapped for their freshwater ice. This industry faded by the 1920s with the advent of refrigeration. A racially and ethnically diverse group of local workers, including the Polish and Irish, found off-season employment in the brickyards. Rockland's location proved advantageous in reducing meltage, a critical factor in determining margins of profit.[11]

Ice and bricks are the most vivid nineteenth-century examples of the commodity exchange between Rockland County and the great urban emporium to the south, but they are not the only ones. Lumbering and sawmills supported the local shipbuilding industry, which provided the sloops and steamboats for river commerce. Ironworks, paper and fiber production, the chemical and textile industry in Garnerville, and leather goods, including shoes (Nyack was known as "Shoetown") were the elements of a broad industrial base. These economic activities strengthened the ties between city and country, not just in the exchange of goods but also in the gradual recognition that while they constituted separate worlds with different ways of life, their borders were becoming more permeable.

FARMING

From the Dutch farmers of the seventeenth century to the truck farmers of the late twentieth, agriculture has been formative in the history of Rockland County. Early farm life centered around the production of fruit, meat, vegetables, butter, eggs, and homespun textiles. As farmers moved from subsistence to surplus production in the late eighteenth and early nineteenth centuries, they were increasingly drawn into the cash nexus of the urban centers, which depended initially on water routes. Railroads opened newer markets, but also increased competition

Concklin Farm, Pomona, NY, 1925; Emma and George Concklin spraying apples *HSRC Collection*

(top) Concklin Farm, Pomona, NY, 1924; George and Howard (on ladder), Emma, Edwin (on ladder), Oscar, and Gordon *HSRC Collection*

(middle) Concklin Farm, Emma Concklin, 1921 *HSRC Collection*

(botttom) Concklin Farm, the four boys, 1926 *HSRC Collection*

from other regions and over time enticed the next generation off the farms to the life of the big city.

Many of these farms were family owned and operated, some with histories reaching back to the Dutch colonial era. The roster includes Concklin, Cropsey, Davies, Duryea, Erickson, Schimpf, Van Houten, and Van Riper—all with multiple generations of workers, bound to the land and living by the rhythms of the seasons.

County agricultural fairs first appeared in 1843. Spring Valley, New City, and Orangeburg served as hosts. By 1860, county fairs were flourishing far across the state, "instructing, educating, and amusing" farmers and the public. New York State underwrote these events through the County Agricultural Society in an effort to stabilize funding.[12] Rockland's fairs emphasized agricultural education and innovation and celebrated farm crafts through competition and prizes. Jellies, jams, pickles, and baked goods lent a domestic air.[13] The addition of bicycles, automobiles, and carnival amusements catered more to urban visitors, and the recreational and nostalgic elements became dominant. But the county fairs remained powerful symbols of rural life.

When The Historical Society of Rockland County honored these farming families in 1999, many agreed with the sentiments of New City's Jim Cropsey: "I live and breathe it . . . there is a great sense of accomplishment and pride when you look at your fields and see something you planted coming in." George Smith of New City lamented the emptiness "when you pull up and leave." The pressure to sell intensified after the Tappan Zee Bridge opened in 1955, accelerating the persistent decline of the previous half-century. The 400 farms alive in 1950 dwindled to 100 by 1969 and to eight 20 years later. The embattled farmers complained that real estate brokers poured in like locusts, encouraged by the practice of rezoning farms as residential because of septic requirements (this made it easier to change residential to business zoning later). Raymond Concklin of Pomona watched as farms became subdivisions. Niles Davies of Congers witnessed the diminishing rural environment and the encroaching suburban landscape. Like any good farmer, he frequently looked to the sky "to check the weather—he may see clouds or he may see golf balls flying from the course across the street." If he looked around the county, he would notice not only the increasing number of golf courses but also the disappearing inventory of remaining farms—only eight at century's end, a barely visible remnant of the 1,000 that shaped the Rockland landscape at the beginning of the century.

What was at stake here was larger than agricultural production and the plight of Rockland farmers. The rural character of the community of multigenerational farmers, with its ties to the land, the clock of nature, hard work, and simplic-

(top left) Program of the 44th Annual Rockland County Industrial Association Fair and Exposition, 1923 *HSRC Collection*

(top right) First Premium Ribbon from 1911 Rockland County Industrial Association Fair and Exposition *HSRC Collection*

(middle) Postcard of the New City fairgrounds during the Rockland County Industrial Association Fair and Exposition, 1910 *HSRC Collection*

(bottom) Postcard of Central Avenue, Pearl River, NY *HSRC Collection*

ity, constituted a worldview. Empathy with nature was the informing idea for a community respectful of tradition and cautious about change. The landscape was encoded with the kinds of values that for two centuries had attracted utopian reformers, religious communities, gentlemen farmers, artists, and writers. They found this space hospitable to their individuality and respectful of their varied aspirations. Its insulation from the rest of the world contributed to a sense of regional identity and secured for Rockland County a distinctive character.[14]

RURAL SANCTUARY

Rockland's rural character, combining a sense of both isolation and accessibility, attracted utopian reformers in search of havens for new ideas and space for their community building. In the nineteenth century, the utopian impulse reached Rockland. In 1826, inspired by a Robert Owen lecture, attorney Henry Fay, Jacob Peterson, George Houston, and Robert L. Jennings, members of the New York Society for Promoting Communities and adherents of socialist ideas that had shaped New Harmony in Indiana in 1825, established the Franklin Community in Haverstraw to "better the conditions of themselves and their fellow men," which they believed could be done by "living in community, having all things in common, giving equal rights to each, and abolishing the terms mine and thine."[15]

They purchased 130 acres from John I. Suffern and by subscription membership grew to 80 participants. The community was organized around a so-called "Church of Reason," which had neither religious ceremonies nor articles of faith. Farming and some mechanical activities promised self-sufficiency and many thought the experiment would succeed. However, internal quarreling and charges of corruption broke up Franklin in a few months.[16] A second, more successful attempt at utopian community building occurred a century later, in 1926. It was organized around the ideas of Rudolf Steiner and anthroposophy—the belief that the nature of man could connect with a comprehensible spiritual world, which would lead to deeper personal development. After World War I, the movement focused on schools, farms, and medical clinics.

In the 1920s, Rudolf Steiner gave a series of lectures that formed the basis for the modern organic farming movement called biodynamic agriculture. A disciple, Ehrenfried Pfeiffer, organized the Threefold Community of South Spring Valley, now Chestnut Ridge, in 1926. The organizers saw the soil and the farm as living organisms, whose maintenance was a basic necessity for survival. Preservation of the soil was essential for the future and was part of the notion of the farm as a self-contained, growing individual entity. The Threefold Community and Threefold Farm have been farmed continuously ever since, using the biodynamic method.[17] The present community includes the Waldorf School, The Pfeiffer Center for environmental education and biodynamic agriculture, Eurythmy Spring Valley for movement art, and the Durie farm.

Among the early twentieth-century urban migrants to Rockland County was New Yorker Ralph Borsodi, who by the age of twenty-two was personally testing the idea of moving "back to the land" and the concept of "voluntary simplicity." In 1920, he bought seven acres and a farm in Suffern, where he launched his experiment in agrarianism for commuters. He described his initial year as an agricultural pioneer:

> Before the end of the first year, the year of the depression in 1921, when millions were tramping the streets of our cities looking for work, we began to enjoy the feeling of plenty which the city-dweller never experiences. We cut our hay; gathered our fruit; made gallons and gallons of cider. We had a cow, and produced our own milk and butter, but finally gave her up. By furnishing us twenty quarts of milk a day she threatened to put us in the dairy business. So we changed to a pair of blooded Swiss goats. We equipped a poultry-yard, and had eggs, chickens, and fat roast capons. We ended the year with plenty not only for our own needs but for a generous hospitality to our friends—some of whom were out of work—a hospitality which, unlike city hospitality, did not involve purchasing everything we served our guests.[18]

He dreamed of being self-supporting and in 1924 acquired a larger farm in what is now Airmont. The new home, built efficiently and economically on concrete slab and with available fieldstones, was soon followed by five other buildings that constituted an estate called Dogwoods. From there he launched his attack on industrial civilization and its noise, filth, and degradation of workers.

In 1933, he offered an alternative to modern industrial living with the publication of *Flight from the City,* which called for a return to the land and championed the virtues of self-sufficiency—an idea popular in the midst of the uncertainties of the Great Depression.[19]

In his preface Borsodi laid out his argument:

> We are living in one of the most interesting periods in the world's history. Industrial civilization is either on the verge of collapse or of rebirth on a new social basis. Men and women who desire to escape from dependence upon the present industrial system and who have no desire to substitute for it depen-

Leaflet describing the Van Houten Fields Association *HSRC Collection*

dence upon a state-controlled system, are beginning to experiment with a way of living which is neither city life nor farm life, but which is an effort to combine the advantages and to escape the disadvantages of both. Reports of the Department of Agriculture call attention to the revival of handicraft industries—the making of rugs and other textiles, furniture, baskets and pottery—for sale along the roads, in near-by farmers' markets, or for barter for other products for the farm and home.[20]

In 1935, Borsodi organized the Bayard Lane community on Route 202 in Suffern within what is today the village of Montebello, with a School of Living; twenty families from New York City began attending regularly, spending weekends there. He used a land trust—Independence Foundation—as a banking and credit institution to underwrite others who wished to build homesteads in the community.

Van Houten Fields, a larger full-scale cooperative, followed shortly after in 1937 and attracted artists, writers, actors, musicians, and craftsmen, who in time acquired the rights to own their own homes.[21]

Borsodi was building on the legacy of the Country Life movement of the turn-of-the-century Progressives, which seemed to promise not only a return to rural nature but also independence and self-sufficiency. His program offered a decentralized alternative life plan that became increasingly attractive in the era of the New Deal and the persistent depression.

These examples, spanning two centuries, reflect a hospitable Rockland landscape that welcomed those in search of a more perfect way of life, confident that the rural environment was both moral and healthful.

In June 1894, the steamboat *Chrystenah* began carrying "tenement waifs" from New York to Nyack, where the children were taken by horse-drawn wagonettes to Mount Lawn, an estate above Upper Nyack. Louis Klopsch, publisher of *The Christian Herald*, established a summer home there as a respite from the appalling living conditions on New York's Lower East Side. In 1898 the program was incorporated as the Christian Herald Children's Home; each summer it served 2,000 to 3,000 boys and girls. In 1905, Jacob Riis, the great Progressive muckraker and author of the *How the Other Half Lives*, helped dedicate the Children's Temple there to provide a prayerful escape from the poor living conditions of the city.[22]

Religious denominations found in Rockland not only a safe haven for children but also a secure place for their denominational homes and centers for religious education. In 1884, the Dominican Congregation of Our Lady of the Rosary, charged with the care of destitute children, purchased the Johnson farm in Sparkill to serve as a Home and School for Boys. By 1889, eleven buildings were added, and in 1895, the community's motherhouse. In 1954, St. Thomas Aquinas College was opened on the property.[23]

Jews came to Rockland in small numbers as early as the 1830s and concentrated in Nyack and Haverstraw, opening hotels and shops. By the end of the century, the numbers were sufficient to establish a Jewish Society in Nyack in 1870 and a Congregation in 1890. The nucleus of the Spring Valley community grew around the 1896 opening of Charles Falkenberg's shirt factory. Jacob Mendelson, who transported much of the original machinery to Spring Valley, induced dozens of eager-for-work immigrants from the Lower East Side to return with him to Rockland County. The enterprising Mendelson converted a farmhouse into summer rooms and added bungalows with lake swimming to create one of the first Jewish vacation retreats. The demand for housing spurred the development of a Jewish residential community on "The Hill" east of Spring Valley's Main Street in 1894.[24] This migration pattern depended on a key individual who linked city and country, publicized Rockland's advantages for Jews, and promised a secure and safe haven for those looking for a new beginning. This model served many subsequent groups, and with only modest alterations has been a persistent paradigm for Rockland County's population expansion.

Word of Rockland spread among Jewish communities in New York City; new opportunities called. Max Auerbach and Murray Rosner in the teens and Louis Bader and Louis Singer in the 1920s opened hotels, the foundation of a burgeoning Jewish resort industry centered in Spring Valley. Thousands came as Spring Valley began to compete with the Catskills. Bungalow colonies flourished as weekend stays extended into summer-long vacations and matured into year-round tourism. This progressive and expanding experience encouraged the establishment of schuls and synagogues, hallmarks of a rooted community.[25] Vacation interludes provided an experiential bond with this place, situating Rockland in the imagination of many New York Jews as a potential permanent residence—their own suburban home. In one of the interesting turns of history, many of the hotels and bungalow communities were the imprint for later housing developments, including low-cost public housing.

PARK AND RIDE

In 1910, the Palisades Interstate Park Commission (PIPC), formed in 1900 to protect the Palisades along the Hudson's western shore, received a gift from Mrs. Mary Williamson Averell Harriman of 10,000 acres in memory of her husband. This provided the foundation for the 50,000-acre Bear Mountain and Harriman state parks. In 1915, the Bear Mountain Inn was opened, including a restaurant, a cafeteria, overnight accommodations in a rustic setting, and a dock for steamboat landings. The inn and the park were also accessible by automobile via Route 9W. This protected natural landscape was the beginning of an expanding park system at the edge of metropolitan New York, providing urbanites with an accessible and healthy respite from the miasmic and crowded city. PIPC's role as a safety valve for urban congestion was an informing idea of the park from its inception. It drew city dwellers to Rockland and solidified the county's reputation as a rural sanctuary. As the number of visitors increased, knowledge of the region spread beyond urban elites, artists, writers, and utopian reformers to the masses in search of recreation and the great escape.

Long and inconvenient steamboat and ferry journeys, winding roadways, and slow-moving traffic overwhelmed local hotels, at times transforming automobiles into improvised bedrooms. If ready access to the new parks was the objective, then travel needed to be more efficient and direct. Plans for a suspension bridge three and a half miles north of Peekskill, linking Anthony's Nose on the east

Steamship *Albany* of the Hudson River Day Line. The *Albany* was in operation from 1800 to circa 1929. *HSRC Collection*

to Fort Montgomery on the west, were approved in 1922. The structure, which would be built of steel to keep costs down and could be completed within three years, drew the ire of critics for whom concrete, because of its massive look and reassuring density, was the only appropriate material. The aesthetic argument was grounded in the notion that the Hudson River required special consideration and that a bridge was not just a roadway, a connector between two points, but needed to harmonize with its river setting. The Bear Mountain toll bridge, the longest suspension bridge at the time, opened in 1924. In spite of its low cost—as late as the 1950s, the toll was only 25 cents for a car and five cents for a pedestrian— and the large crowds crossing to Bear Mountain, it proved a financial disaster for many years.[26]

However, the Bear Mountain Bridge brought more urbanites into contact with Rockland, reinforced its attractiveness as a vacation spot, and established the first bridge link between Westchester and Rockland counties. In the subsequent debates about the Tappan Zee Bridge, the Bear Mountain Bridge would serve as a reference point for both sides, and when the George Washington Bridge was completed, it was fixed as the northern frame for the planners.

Rockland County had a long pre-automobile history as a vacation destination

From a high point, showing the Hudson River at the southern gateway of the Highlands.

SCENIC MOUNTAIN TRIPS
Conducted by the Palisades Interstate Park

Busses, starting from Bear Mountain Grove, return in time for boat departure.

On the Park Drive—Scenic trips are over roads like this.

The Park Commission supplies free boats on Hessian Lake, where 100 Hessian soldiers were drowned in the Revolutionary War.

The Popolopen Creek Viaduct connecting the Revolutionary Forts Clinton and Montgomery.

Series of postcards showing tours at Bear Mountain State Park (from top to bottom) circa 1915, 1916, and 1917
HSRC Collection

The Kanohwahke Chain of Lakes en route to Lake Stahahe—a trip of two hours.

Stahahe Lake, the most beautiful lake in the Ramapos—end of the two-hour trip.

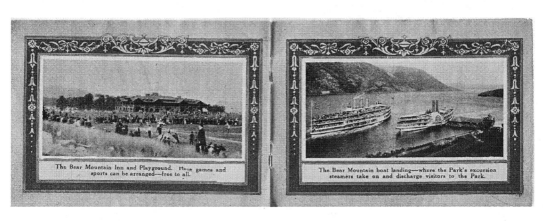

The Bear Mountain Inn and Playground. Here games and sports can be arranged—free to all.

The Bear Mountain boat landing—where the Park's excursion steamers take on and discharge visitors to the Park.

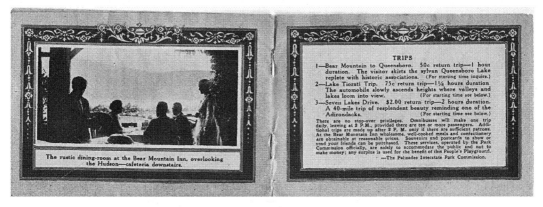

The rustic dining-room at the Bear Mountain Inn, overlooking the Hudson—cafeteria downstairs.

TRIPS

1—Bear Mountain to Queensboro. 50c return trip—1 hour duration. The visitor skirts the sylvan Queensboro Lake replete with historic associations. (For starting time inquire.)

2—Lake Tiorati Trip. 75c return trip—1¼ hours duration. The automobile slowly ascends heights where valleys and lakes loom into view. (For starting time see below.)

3—Seven Lakes Drive. $2.00 return trip—2 hours duration. A 40-mile trip of resplendent beauty reminding one of the Adirondacks. (For starting time see below.)

There are no stop-over privileges. Omnibusses will make one trip daily, leaving at 2 P.M., provided there are ten or more passengers. Additional trips are made up after 2 P.M. only if there are sufficient patrons. At the Bear Mountain Inn wholesome, well-cooked meals and confectionery are obtainable at reasonable prices. Souvenirs and postcards to show or send your friends can be purchased. These services, operated by the Park Commission officially, are solely to accommodate the public and not to make money; any surplus is used for the benefit of this People's Playground.

—The Palisades Interstate Park Commission.

Series of postcards showing tours at Bear Mountain State Park (from top to bottom) circa 1918, 1919, and 1920
HSRC Collection

The steamer
Washington Irving,
in use from 1913 to 1926
HSRC Collection

Postcard of
Bear Mountain Bridge
HSRC Collection

Postcard of
Bear Mountain Bridge
and State Park *HSRC Collection*

Hessian Lake, Bear Mountain State Park *HSRC Collection*

and Piermont become one of the attractive summer escapes for urbanites. Accessible by steamboat and rail, it offered leafy hillsides, river views, resort hotels, bathing pavilions, and ice cream parlors. The centerpiece of the resort community was the Fort Comfort Inn, which advertised "high-class service, beautiful surroundings, caters especially to tourists."[27] A three-story annex was added but was destroyed by fire in 1912. To complement the inn, the Fort Comfort Resort Park was opened on the peninsula near the river; it included a bathing beach, a merry-go-round, a dance hall, boating, and river excursions. *The Nyack Piermont Directory* of 1902 advertised the Fort Comfort Beach as

> the most desirable place on the Hudson for bathing and has many attractive features not found at seaside resorts. The clean fine sand bottom sloping gradually for a long distance makes it absolutely safe for small children and enjoyable to all. A modern Bathing Pavilion lighted by electricity for bathing at night, has about one hundred large booths furnished with shower and foot baths.[28]

Summer vacations are the halfway house of suburbanization. They provided families with a safe way to test country living under the most propitious conditions. Suffern, a key station on the Erie Line with twenty trains a day, attracted

Postcard showing the *Chrystenah* docked at Rockland Lake *HSRC Collection*

some travelers with its Victorian depot and "romantic scenery, fascinating beauty and rich land."[29] Resort hotels and boarding houses provided affluent and increasingly mobile middle-class New Yorkers with an introduction to Rockland. Many returned summer after summer; some, like Thomas Fortune Ryan, built vacation "cottages" like Montebello, a country estate, and others, fully smitten, established permanent residences.

GETTING THERE

Ferries were the lifeline of many river villages. Their changing size, shape, and speed embodied three centuries of maritime engineering innovation. Three routes linked the east and west shores: Yonkers to Alpine, Dobbs Ferry to Sneden's Landing, and Tarrytown to Nyack. The oldest service, from Dobbs Ferry to Sneden's Landing, was started by William Dobbs, a local fisherman/farmer who began ferrying people across in 1729. He relinquished control to the Snedens, who persisted with the service into the early twentieth century.

The vibrant trade between Tarrytown and Nyack had long depended on regular ferry service. George W. B. Gedney was granted by Rockland County Court of Common Pleas the first ferry franchise between Nyack and Tarrytown in 1839. Usage increased, and a demand for larger vessels led to the *Tappan Zee* (1878) being replaced by the revered *Rockland*. Its large capacity enabled it to transport automobiles and its improved maneuverability avoided the Tappan Zee's sand-

Notice of the steamboat *Nyack*, 1827 *HSRC Collection*

Steamer *Highlander*, c. 1900 *HSRC Collection*

The *Rockland* ferry between Nyack and Tarrytown, c. 1915
HSRC Collection

Undated photograph of the Piermont Pier
HSRC Collection

bars. The long-running vessel acquired a folk history centered on Captain John Lyon and crewman John Rice. Price wars, ferry races, and contested leases marked Lyon's stormy tenure until he died in 1923. Then the North Ferry Company took over and provided service until 1941, after which it fell on hard times, a casualty of the newly completed George Washington Bridge.[30]

Among the groups in search of a haven were itinerant "Gypsies" who passed

(top) Bessie Clarke, Sparkill, NY, in her car, 1914 (bottom) 1915 *HSRC Collection*

through Rockland in the late 1800s and early 1900s and encamped in the summer in Central Nyack, Spring Valley, and Haverstraw. They traded horses to the brick-yard owners, for towing brick sleds and loaded wagons. They sold and refinished pots and pans and did small tasks for local farmers. They participated in the Or-angeburg Fair on their way to the big Danbury Fair in Connecticut.[31]

In 1890, most Rocklanders got around the county by horse. But by the second decade of the twentieth century the main streets of many towns were crowded with automobiles. Dirt roads rutted by wagon wheels and free-for-all driving, un-checked by traffic lights, contributed to the sense of chaos. This also highlighted the poor conditions of Rockland's roads.

The role of bridges in organizing an inchoate road system cannot be underesti-mated as a prerequisite for Rockland's development. In 1916 the dangerous gorge at Popolopen Creek in Orange County and, shortly after, the chasm at Sparkill Creek were spanned as the county took its first steps toward a modern transpor-tation system. More bridges followed.[32]

The automobile diminished the central importance of the village. Stores and factories were now liberated from the necessity of having to be in the same neighborhood as their customers and workers. Signs of this new mobility were clear in the 1920s, as riverfront villages like Nyack saw the Hudson not as a vital communication link but rather as an obstacle to greater mobility and easier travel.[33] The automobile was compelling a new view of the county and its geography. Now its rural insularity was being challenged.

ARTISTS AND WRITERS

Maxwell Anderson moved to New York City in 1918 and found writing jobs at the *New Republic* and *The World*, where a friend induced him to stay for one year in Grand View, an upstate community increasingly attractive to New York artists and writers. He returned to Rockland three years later, in 1922, to what would eventually be a permanent residence on South Mountain Road in New City. There, surrounded by large operating farms, he and two friends purchased a large parcel with three houses that they divided among themselves. Anderson selected the house overlooking a deep, wide ravine with a waterfall fed by a large brook. His move to South Mountain, known as "The Road" among the locals, proved to be the most creative moment in his life and enabled him to move from journalism to playwriting. According to his son, "the nomadic pattern was broken."[34]

For the next thirty years, while reshaping his house and land, including the addition of "Anderson's pond," he produced dozens of plays, including twenty-eight Broadway productions. The merging of place and work in his life deepened his affection for the region and his neighbors, farmers and artists alike. This bond with the land he shared with his friends, including art-

Undated photograph of Maxwell Anderson *HSRC Collection*

Undated photograph of Maxwell Anderson *Courtesy of Billy Rose Theatre Division, The New York Public Library for the Performing Arts, Astor, Lenox and Tilden Foundations*

Taken from High Tor, looking south, 1984 *HSRC Collection*

ist Henry Varnum Poor, sculptor/painter Hugo Robus, film director John House-
man, designer Ruth Reeves, illustrators Milton Caniff and Bill Maudlin, and later
actor Burgess Meredith and composer Kurt Weill. They constituted a critical
mass of like-minded individuals who drew comfort and inspiration from "The
Road," where the line between life and work was blurred and the landscape was
cast in a special aura.

It is not surprising then that Anderson would become a vigilant and staunch
defender of the land. When the Rockland Power and Light Company attempted
to string electric lines over his home and his waterfall, he was duly provoked
and declared war on the surveyors, targeting their stakes and markers, which
he removed under cover of darkness. This response would be emulated in the
next decade by opponents of the Tappan Zee Bridge, who routed the surveyors
from their property. What Anderson and his artist allies and neighbors saw was
an incursion of the modern world and the march of progress, which threatened
their self-imposed and carefully nurtured rustic enclosure. This was not simply a
question of overhead power lines but a first assault on their carefully constructed
environment.

In the early spring of 1936, Anderson climbed the 832-foot peak of High Tor,
the northernmost point of the Palisades. This was a spot favored by the artist
community on "The Road" for its remarkable views of the Hudson, Rockland
County, and the Highlands. From the summit, the Tarrytown General Motors
automobile plant came into view to the east, and as he looked down, he could
see Route 9W hugging the river's edge and carrying the George Washington
Bridge traffic into his neighborhood. He was poised between two worlds—his
bucolic South Mountain and the fast-encroaching modern technology with its

advance party, the great urban migration. This primal struggle between the forces of preservation and progress was vividly documented as he looked south and grimaced at the deep gouges on the back of Middle Mountain, the work of the insatiable quarrymen. He was overcome by a wave of deep anxiety, knowing that the New York Trap Rock Company was after High Tor, pressuring its owner, Elmer Van Orden, to sell. Tough and independent, Van Orden resisted, aided in imagination by the ghosts of the past that inhabited the region and guarded its history. These two life forces were now fully engaged and, as in a battle of ancient chthonic gods, the outcome seemed uncertain.[35]

Anderson translated this real-life drama into melodrama and used his art to defend his life's place. In January 1937, the struggle at High Tor was transformed into a Broadway play in which Dutch and Indian characters and the ghosts of High Tor do battle with Biggs and Skimmerhorn, stand-ins for the traprock company. Van Van Dorn, the owner of the land, finally agrees to sell, heeding the advice of an old sachem: "Our god is now the setting sun, and we must follow it. For other races out of the east will live here in their time, one following another. Each will build its cities . . . but none will live forever. . . . Let them come despoiling (for) these will not endure."[36]

The play's outcome suggests resignation in the face of the inevitable forces of modernization; indeed, Anderson himself eventually left South Mountain Road and Rockland County for Connecticut (and then California). However, in reality, High Tor was preserved, in no small part thanks to the interest and support generated by the play. The Committee to Save High Tor was organized by the Rockland County Conservation Association with Anderson, who served as honorary chairman. In a letter to Collis P. Huntington, Anderson framed the issue: "High Tor is on the market . . . it could be a state park—or the quarry could buy it. Probably it's no use trying to hold back the march of industrial machinery, but if you want to give a chunk of that sum I think I could raise the rest."[37]

Rockland County Conservation Association letter raising funds to buy High Tor, signed by Mary Mowbray-Clarke *HSRC Collection*

Scene from Maxwell Anderson's play *High Tor* *Courtesy of Billy Rose Theatre Division, The New York Public Library for the Performing Arts, Astor, Lenox and Tilden Foundations*

Anderson helped the grassroots effort to raise the money, purchase the mountain, and donate it to the Palisades Interstate Park Commission in 1943. Isabelle Savell, the writer/historian/environmentalist of Grand View, observed that High Tor "is a symbol, and a mystical one at that, that . . . holds the loyalties and concerns of the countryside." In the Anderson play, Van complains to Biggs and Skimmerhorn that he "wants to have it back the way it was before you came."[38] It meant something to the locals, to who they were, and to their definition of Rockland. This mountain had become part of the Hudson Valley's great preserved landscape of nostalgia.[39] In the name of preservation and conservation, Anderson and his fellow city expats hoped to maintain the world of the 1920s, one they had come to cherish and identify as rural. They sought to fix the landscape in time, a determination that reflected their own mental map rather than the attitudes of the true locals.

This fundamental struggle between preservation and progress would provide the vocabulary for the ensuing battles over the Tappan Zee Bridge. Anderson was able to articulate in *High Tor* the sense of foreboding that informed his feelings about the inevitability of change and the ominous future threatening the landscape he had come to revere and love. The intuition, at times self-serving, of danger in the scale and scope of progress was a prescient guide to the future of Rockland County.

CROSSING THE HUDSON

The idea of a bridge across the Hudson had teased the imagination of Rocklanders for over a century. As early as 1866, the weekly *Rockland County Journal* reported a fictitious story about a bill to construct a bridge across the Hudson, between Tarrytown and Nyack. With the help of divine intervention, the bill was passed and the bridge was completed in 48 hours on January 7–8, 1866, permitting droves of cattle, sleighs, and even a steam boiler to cross safely.[40] Beyond

Car crossing the Hudson River between Nyack and Tarrytown, circa 1923 *HSRC Collection*

The "Ice Bridge"—the frozen Hudson River and crossing from Nyack to Tarrytown *HSRC Collection*

this local fantasy, many talked about the ice bridge that returned most winters. Local papers chronicled the advance of the ice and announced "The Tappan Zee bridge—of ice, will be ready for crossing in a few days." A few weeks later it would be noted that "Hundreds of people have crossed the ice bridge between Nyack and Tarrytown."[41] A folk history grew, chronicling the unique ways people got across. Two Tarrytown Boy Scouts on bicycles tied ropes to their sled and pulled their sister across the river to her job as a teacher in Rockland's Spring Valley. This was an improvement over their father's walk across the river from Tarrytown to Spring Valley, a 10-mile trip, which began at 3:00 p.m. and ended with his return home by 11:00 p.m.[42] The ice bridge took courage and fortitude and must have stimulated thoughts of an easier, truly year-round crossing.

One of the earliest proposals, in 1905, centered on the Erie Railroad at Piermont and the possibility that the company would build a bridge to connect with the New York Central Railroad on the Westchester side and run trains into Grand Central Station, the above-ground predecessor of the present terminal.[43] As speculation grew, land prices soared, and it was reported that a Mrs. Austin Abbot of Palisades received $40,000 more for her property than she had expected to obtain; real estate agents talked about increased sales in Sparkill and in various neighborhoods along the Palisades.[44] This early boom exemplified the close connection between a Hudson River bridge and land and housing values.

In 1919 G. Briggs Buchanan, president of the Rockland County Good Roads Association, endorsed a bridge spanning the Hudson from Rockland to Westchester and committed his association to do its "utmost to forward this endeavor."[45] This association would be the voice for the automobile industry, drivers, and better roads throughout the period. The automobile, and its organized lobbyists, had become a new force in determining transportation planning in the region.

The importance of improved transportation was also crucial to west side farmers, for whom a bridge would open the richest market in the world. They complained that from New York City to Albany, a distance of 150 miles, there were no spans crossing the river, only antiquated ferries. Two thirds of the state's population and key businesses were on the east side, while raw materials for manufacture and agricultural products were located on the west side. When the river was frozen or stormy, ferries did not run; understandably, farmers pleaded for competitive access to New York City.[46]

In an effort to cash in on the suburban boom of the 1920s, the Rockland Realty Board urged a prompt decision on the plan to span the Hudson from Fort Washington to New Jersey (the George Washington Bridge). Theodore Waters of Tallman, director of the Rockland County Realty Board, commented that "Rockland offered many opportunities for home development . . . and it will be the most

Sales flyer for large home in Grand View
along the river, circa 1930 *HSRC Collection*

Booklet produced by the Rockland County
Realty Board extolling Rockland County,
circa 1930 *HSRC Collection*

sought-after home community." He urged the public to disregard the opposition
to the bridge's placement—some argued that it would ruin views of the Palisades
or transportation companies would be curtailed if a bridge went through. He also
noted that the "county has by no means received its quota of people from New
York City . . . it has all and more than any other section—cheaper lands, more
beautiful scenery and better health giving qualities."[47] This sense of Rockland as
a suburb-in-waiting would be a persistent theme for the voices promoting progress. The conviction grew that the only thing holding the county back was lack of
a Hudson River bridge.

To implement Waters's boosterism, the Realty Board established an information bureau "to give unbiased information about Rockland County as a whole,"
so that potential home buyers could make comparisons to "Long Island, Westchester, New Jersey, Connecticut and Staten Island." In a most telling argument,
Waters exposed the raw nerve of the progress argument: "Rockland has been the
most backward of all the New York commuting sections, first, because the people,
living comfortably under old-fashioned standards, have not been anxious to have
the crowd come in and cause a change. Second, because insufficient transportation facilities compared with other sections have kept the people away."[48]

Transportation limitations were clearly secondary in the argument from the larger cultural view that Rockland was a metropolitan backwater that needed to be updated and modernized. Yet this very "backwardness" was what appealed to many urbanites exhausted by the burdens of fast-paced modern city life. Ironically, in the same breath Waters acknowledged this, noting that Rockland was "the last frontier of country life located within the New York commuting zone."[49]

Between 1929 and 1931, after seven years of study, the Regional Planning Authority (RPA) published a ten-volume *Regional Plan for New York*, laying out designs for a vast organic city, within a state "girdled by rail and highway loops."[50] The new metropolis of the future, or at least 1965, would have a population of 20 million, to be served by an integrated system of highways, railways, commuter rapid-transit lines, parkways, and a ring of parks. New bridges and tunnels would cross the Hudson, Harlem, and East rivers, as well as the Narrows and New York harbor. The *Regional Plan* included 47 proposals, many for highways and river crossings, with detailed maps extending outward in a 50-mile radius from New York City.

Some typical parkway routes proposed for Rockland included one from Suffern along the Ramapo River and through the Palisades Interstate Park to Bear Mountain. *Regional Plan* maps showed a connecting link through Rockland and into Putnam County and a proposed tunnel under the Hudson River to connect with the Northern Railroad of New Jersey (Erie Railroad system) near Sparkill.

The goal was to relieve concentration of the population in the congested city center—Manhattan—by coordinated planning, interconnected transportation, and newly designed vertical cities. Horizontal development was the enemy, for it carried the threat of sprawl and the loss of open space so critical "for the health of the inhabitants and the beauty of their surroundings."[51] The series of parks and parkways in the outer loop would provide access to open spaces, and Rockland's rural character would determine its function and future. The proposed new highway and river tunnels would serve to ease the movement to and from the parklands of the outer ring. While new residential development was planned for Westchester, none was offered for Rockland, in the hope of preserving it as rural/park space.[52]

This RPA plan for a "landscape of modernity" depended on a well-organized and tightly integrated rail system. However, most of the municipal and county-proposed projects depended on highways, which ironically facilitated the automobile suburbs and their by-product, sprawl. The *Regional Plan* opposition to mass suburbanization of the working class, premature subdivisions, and the proliferation of small houses was undercut by these local plans and the Port Authority's abandonment of railways for highways, which encouraged the desire for the

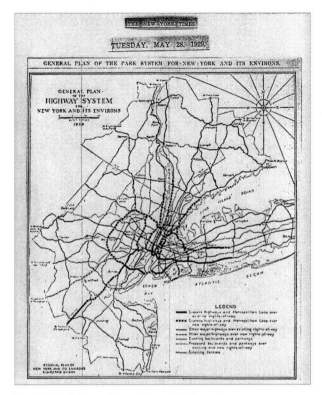

The New York Times General Plan of Highway Systems

Courtesy Craig H. Long. Reprinted with permission, The New York Times

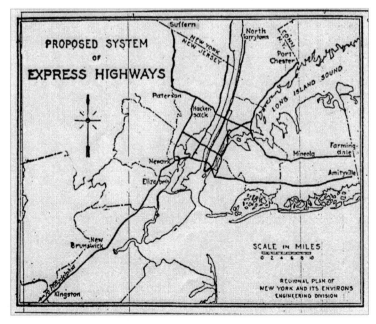

The New York Times Proposed System of Highways   *Courtesy Craig H. Long.*

Reprinted with permission, The New York Times

Piermont Pier, before Camp Shanks *HSRC Collection*

single-family home.[53] The RPA hoped to maintain the functional integrity of each of its proposed zones, but subsequent actions of regional government agencies encouraged and initiated the changes in infrastructure that were the prerequisites for mass suburbanization and the transformation of Rockland County.

The *Regional Plan*, the dramatic increase in automobile registrations, and talk of the new Hudson River crossing at Fort Lee instigated a series of new bridge proposals.[54] Sensing momentum in the building boom in Westchester's towns and villages, five weekly Rockland newspapers offered plans to build a bridge across the Hudson at Dobbs Ferry; others suggested a Hook Mountain structure from Goat Mountain to Tarrytown Heights.[55]

In Rockland, Democratic New York Assemblyman Ferdinand (Fred) R. Horn Jr. emerged as the leader of the bridge boosters. He drafted a bill in 1930 for a new bridge at Piermont, picking up on an idea that the PIPC had studied for some time. Horn was the first to come forward with a plan for a toll bridge. New highways would have to be constructed on both sides of the river and Route 9W widened.[56] Horn argued that the George Washington and Bear Mountain bridges did not serve Rockland, and he recommended several possible crossing points, at Dobbs Ferry and Sneden's Landing or Hastings-on-Hudson and Piermont, and even supported a survey to determine whether or not a tunnel from Piermont to Hastings was technically feasible.[57] The village of Piermont anticipated a boom if Horn's bill was passed; residents welcomed the possibility of better access to Westchester and increased property values.[58]

Horn, who was also a county Realtor, persisted in his commitment to a Hudson River crossing; he moved back and forth between bridge and tunnel, open to many different Rockland sitings. But his primary concern in all his bill-making, lobbying, and public speeches was to link Rockland to "large, wealthy and progressive Westchester."[59] He fought for so long and with such single-mindedness that he won the designation "father of the bridge." Critics disparagingly mocked the idea as "Horn's Folly."

Fred Horn was born in New York in 1897. His father owned a harness and saddle shop in New York and continued to operate the business after the family migrated to Nanuet in 1909. In Rockland Fred worked as a real-estate broker, county clerk, and assemblyman and served as a volunteer fireman. As a Realtor he was a strong advocate of the multiple listing system—a clear growth strategy to accelerate home sales. During his tenure as assemblyman in the 1930s, he was a vocal booster for "glorious Rockland the gateway to the great empire state of New York." He did caution his fellow boosters, however, warning, "as we grow, we must plan."

Horn represented the forces of change hoping to pull a lethargic, laidback Rockland, which some described as backward, into the modern world. Ferry service, according to Horn, "was satisfactory in the slower days but it is subject to too many delays and interruptions for these swift moving days." He believed one of the defining character-

Reelection poster for Ferdinand Horn, circa 1932

HSRC Collection

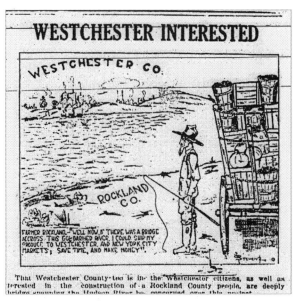

Westchester was seen as a place where Rockland County farmers could sell their goods.

Courtesy Craig H. Long. Reprinted with permission, Rockland County Times

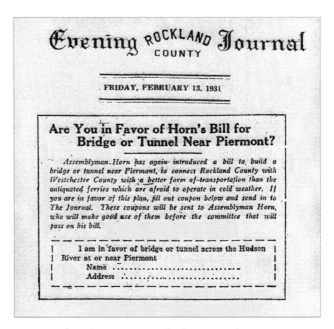

1931 survey form for agreement on bridge or tunnel in Piermont

Courtesy Craig H. Long. Reprinted with permission: The Journal News/Gannett Co. Inc.

istics of the modern world was speed. The key to that was better transportation, which promised a faster and more dependable connection to Westchester and New York City, provided by a bridge or tunnel crossing of the Hudson. Rockland's splendid rural isolation would be broken and the forces of progress unleashed. It was a bold vision in the depths of the depression, but one that in time would garner New Deal federal support. While the issues were grounded in a specific place, they constituted a long and persistent struggle between progress and preservation, the one looking back to an idealized past, the other toward an imagined future. There is no doubt where Fred Horn stood.

In the face of the public silence that seemed to greet Horn's bridge and tunnel proposals, local newspaper editorials urged their readers to "get behind it." Others called for hearty support for Horn's Hudson bill because "it's a great thing for development of Rockland."[60] A coupon poll was initiated by the *Rockland County Evening Journal,* encouraging local residents to send petitions to their legislators urging them to construct a bridge in Piermont: "Sign The Coupon!"[61] Local organizations began to mobilize as Horn's bill gained momentum; bridge committees appeared on both sides of the Hudson. An informal dinner at the Villa Lafayette in Spring Valley produced the first image of a Rockland–Westchester bridge and established a permanent committee while declaring that "the bridge would do for Rockland County what the 'Fort Lee bridge' is doing for Fort Lee."[62]

In the summer of 1930, Governor Roosevelt announced plans for a Mid-Hudson Bridge Authority, which generated a great deal of discussion about the location of the next bridge. The *Evening Journal* announced that the "conquest of the Hudson was just begun, and with the Bear Mountain & Poughkeepsie bridges, it is foreseen that other bridges would follow, perhaps every 25 miles (or) so."[63] It is important to note that the bridging of the Hudson is described in terms of conquest—the mastery of humans over the obstacle of nature with technology as the means and the engineer as the agent.

Horn, undeterred by the defeat of the first bill after Roosevelt announced the Mid-Hudson Bridge Authority, introduced a second bridge proposal (also defeated) and attempted to build local support with another coupon campaign. He arranged a meeting with Governor Roosevelt in March 1931; soon after, a Commission to Study the Plan for the Hudson River Bridge was established. Republican opposition was now galvanized: 1932 was an election year, and Horn was charged with insincerity because he switched bridge locations. He bristled and complained of "unseen powers" that continued to defeat his bills; however, he retained his seat in the Assembly.

The Republicans appealed to David Steinman, consulting engineer on the George Washington Bridge. It was reported that he believed "the Horn Bridge" would be too costly and technically impossible. Steinman noted that the George Washington Bridge span is 500 feet, making it the longest suspension bridge in the world, and the "Horn" bridge would have to cover a distance between 5,000 and 6,000 feet, which would necessitate many piers being built to sustain it. Furthermore, he argued that the War Department in Washington would never give its consent because of navigation concerns.[64]

More dire predictions followed. Critics warned of roads jammed with traffic when the George Washington Bridge opened. Traffic engineers agreed that the highways of Bergen and Rockland counties would be overcrowded with traffic once the motorists began to find their way over the new bridge. Traffic from New York City, Brooklyn, Long Island, and New England would flow over it, traveling west. Charles R. Masten, president of the Bergen County Automobile Club, stated that existing roads were not built to handle this heavy volume and that local municipalities were not prepared. From Bergen the traffic was expected to continue into Rockland, and all New York upstate traffic would go through, using the Franklin Turnpike and Route 17. These traffic concerns were a clear recognition of the correlation between a river crossing and highway capacity, and the expansive network of communities soon to be linked in this emerging metropolitan transportation system. The concerns negatively underlined the shift from rail to auto and the radical departure from the 1929 *Regional Plan*, which called for regions to be linked by the railroad.

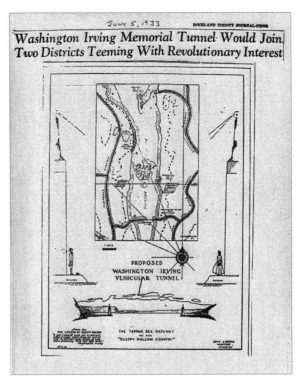

On April 6, 1934, two Conklin boys driving to see the movie *Death Takes a Holiday* were killed on Route 17 at the Suffern bypass, an intersection judged "the most dangerous in the county." The tragic event brought attention to the overburdened Rockland roads crowded with local drivers, commercial vehicles, and travelers passing through. Many residents wondered how much more this inadequate system would be taxed by a river crossing. Two years later, a state department of transportation survey reinforced the findings of the Rockland County Planning Board that Route 17 between Hillburn and Sloatsburg carried more traffic than any other road in the region and was the heaviest traveled road in New York.[65]

The bridge debate was further complicated by jurisdictional questions involving the New York Port Authority and the newly proposed Irvington–Sneden's Landing tunnel, which fell within their domain, south of 41 degrees, 4 minutes longitude (two miles north of the Piermont pier). Below that line the Port Authority held control, and it was not likely to allow another bridge to compete with the George Washington Bridge or any of its other river crossings. This jurisdictional impasse would compel the planners to move north into the Nyack area. This alternate idea did not get much traction and faded quickly.

Undaunted, Horn now advocated another bill, for the Washington Irving Memorial Tunnel, which would join Nyack and Tarrytown, two districts with a common Revolutionary heritage and shared history. South Nyack architect John J. Croke drew up the plans.[66] The use of historic association to link the two counties reflected the 1930s effort to emphasize local and regional history and to imagine highways and bridges as memory markers.

In July 1935, Governor Herbert H. Lehman signed a bill to create the Rockland–Westchester Causeway and Tunnel Authority. Horn was on hand to witness the signing but was not assigned to the authority, which commenced negotiations with the federal Public Works Administration for funds, authorized test borings in the river to establish the terminals, and introduced a bill in Congress to underwrite the construction costs.[67] At a dinner held by civic groups to boost the Hudson span, Clarkstown Supervisor Edward Wells stated that the crossing would bypass New York City and become one of the principal links in a coast-to-coast highway connecting New England with California.[68]

Plans were drafted for a crossing structure at Nyack and a $7 million loan was sought. The state Department of Public Works prepared tentative plans for federal authorities in Washington, confident of approval of the loan by the PWA.[69] In August 1935, the House and Senate passed the Hudson River Bridge bill. All that was needed was the approval of the War Department to ensure the safe navigation of the river.

The bridge now seemed to come to life, and river communities, long apathetic, awakened to the possibility that new access roads could dissect their towns and displace many of their residents. Mayor William B. Page noted that South Nyack's fine residential district was slated for destruction, and he pleaded that the bridge's approach problems not be dumped in his town. Frank R. Crumbie, Mayor of Upper Nyack, felt that the bridge was not an economic necessity and would spoil the view. There were some lonely voices in favor of the bridge, such as Robert Gibson of Tappan, who stated that "a horrible glacial period" separated Rockland and Westchester, and that many times he'd stood on his side of the river and wondered if he could get across because it was blocked with ice, and it would be too late to drive 16 miles downstream to cross there and keep an appointment.[70]

Opposition now began to organize, and a key voice was that of Grand View Zoning Administrator Elmer S. Hader, who criticized plans for a Grand View terminal. Hader stated that "people will continue to oppose a location in South Nyack as much as in their own village. We'll fight until we see the first truck come lumbering across the bridge!"[71] Hader was not all talk. He took his case to the Board of Directors of the Rockland County Conservation Association, suggesting the bridge terminal be located "where it will do the least harm, where it will

Elmer Hader (right), looking over a set of plans, c. 1950 *John F. Geist, photographer. HSRC Collection*

be the most economical to build, and where it will bring the most good to the community." The association decided to send a letter to Assemblywoman Jane Todd of Westchester, asking for particulars on the passage of the bill authorizing the building of the bridge.[72] Speaking in Clarkstown, Hader enumerated the reasons for his opposition: the bridge would be used largely by trucks coming from New England, the exit on the westerly side would bring traffic onto River Road in Grand View, and the widening of Route 9W would create more congestion and present more traffic problems and would destroy the historical Salisbury House. He encouraged the Rockland County Conservation Association to join with the Hudson River Conservation Association to preserve the beauties of the Hudson Valley, in particular, the Tappan Zee.[73]

Surveyors starting to work in the vicinity of the Bight in Grand View were run out of town by Hader and Police Chief Walter Edmonson. Hader explained he would not have gone after them had they not "trespassed" on his property and cut down shrubbery and a mulberry tree for sight lines to Route 9W. Edmonson warned the surveyors not to enter anyone else's property. Hader declared that any resident had the right, in the absence of a court order to the contrary, to keep surveyors off his property, as with other trespassers. Later, at a meeting of the Rockland County Planning Board, he continued to voice his objections, and at his urging the board decided that no recommendations or suggestions on the terminus entrances would be made until a thorough study had been completed.[74]

Hader continued to intensify his attack: "We will keep surveyors for the bridge out of Grand View if we have to deputize every man in the village to prevent their trespassing." Village Trustee Charles C. Ewart, chairman of the police committee of the Board of Trustees, confirmed that special police would be assigned to keep the surveyors out. A resolution by Upper Nyack Trustees stated that the board was "unalterably opposed to the construction of the so-called proposed bridge and/or causeway," believing it would interfere with navigation and "destroy the natural scenic beauties," "disfigure" the Tappan Zee Bay, cause "irreparable injury" to property owners, and lower property values.[75] This growing opposition succeeded temporarily in delaying the contract for the test borings.

Hader's house on River Road in Grand View now became the epicenter of the opposition. One can only imagine the character of the discussion between Elmer and his wife, Berta, who organized other women to prevent surveyors from entering the village. Around 1:00 p.m. on September 12, 1936, Mrs. Hader spotted a group of men who turned out to be surveyors from the office of Colonel Frederick S. Greene, Superintendent of the Department of Public Works. When she found that some of her neighbors were not home, Hader ordered her servants to intercept these intruders. The surveyors refused to identify themselves and said that it was foolish to fight the state.[76] *The New York Times* now referred to the crossing battles as the "Bridge Wars."

Mary Mowbray-Clarke *HSRC Collection, Gift of Alan Anderson*

A meeting at the Nyack YMCA drew 150 bridge opponents, who formed a Rockland County branch of the Hudson River Conservation Association and described the bridge as a "scenic blot." Mary Mowbray-Clarke, landscape consultant, founder of the artists' colony on South Mountain Road in New City, and an outspoken critic of the project was elected president.

A telegram composed by Elmer Hader and signed by more than 400 residents of the Nyacks and Grand View was sent to Governor Lehman, protesting the construction of the Nyack–Tarrytown bridge and urging an inquiry. Signers included Helen Hayes, who owned a mansion in Nyack. The telegram stated,

> Preliminary surveys now in progress indicate that the site selected for this bridge is at a point where the river is three miles wide, where the bridge approaches will disastrously affect extensive property interests and where traffic issuing from the bridge will create very serious problems. Very weighty reasons exist for relocating the bridge, if it is to be built at all, at one of the several points where the width of the river does not exceed one mile and where approaches on both sides will be on State-owned property. May we ask the favor of being informed by you as to whether we may hope for any action toward the inquiry which we hereby request?[77]

In a stroke of bold showmanship, opponents invited Governor Lehman on a ferry ride to see the folly of constructing a bridge where the river was so wide and the Tappan Zee so picturesque. Hader announced more mass meetings, and he sensed that opposition to the bridge was gathering strength.[78] He argued that the planners had looked at the bridge project as engineers, insensitive to the local communities and to what the taxpayers believed.[79]

Berta and Elmer Hader were longtime residents of Grand View. They built their red sandstone house on River Road where they wrote and illustrated over 100 children's books from 1927 to 1964. Several were about life in Rockland County, including *Little Town*, *The Little Stone House*, *Squirrely of Willow Hill*, and *The Big Snow*. Two of their works focus on the Tappan Zee, *The Friendly Phoebe* and *The Runaways*. The Haders, like Horn, were New York City migrants who moved to Rockland in the same decade. And like so many adopted sons, they became passionate Rocklanders. But they looked in different directions—Horn to a future of progress and the Haders to the past and its preservation. In 1947, Berta and Elmer prepared a memoir entitled "Home Sweet Home: How to Get One."[80] It provides a rich and sensitive recollection of their Rockland years—a paean to life in Grand View and Rockland before the war.

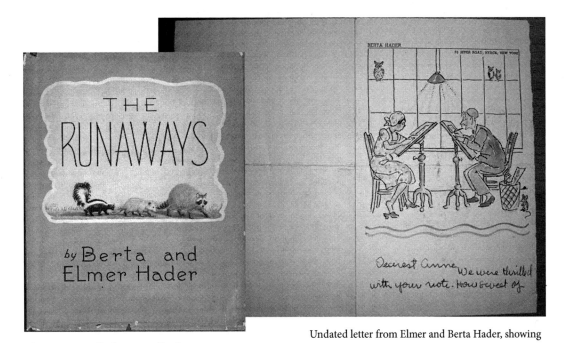

The Runaways tells the story of bridge construction through the eyes of forest animals.
HSRC Collection. Reprinted with permission, Joy Hoerner Rich

Undated letter from Elmer and Berta Hader, showing a watercolor of the two painting *HSRC Collection*

Undated letter from Elmer and Berta Hader. A watercolor portrait of the couple can be seen in the added mirror. *HSRC Collection*

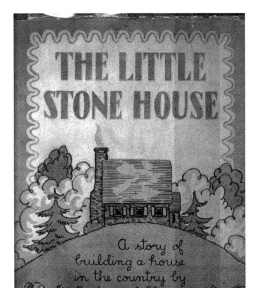

The Haders fictionalized the building of their little stone house in this children's book.
HSRC Collection. Reprinted with permission, Joy Hoerner Rich

They opened the memoir with the words "WE WANT HOUSES," an old cry familiar to those who had lived through the disaster of World War I. "Then as now . . . the need for housing became acute . . . thousands of young married couples in search of . . . houses in the country. Then as now, there were thousands of returning soldiers, people anxious to marry and establish a home." They had a story to tell about their own youthful quest for a home. In 1919, the fighting was over and a domestic battle was taking shape over establishing a family home. They noted that in their early years many of their contemporaries attributed marriage failures to not having a home of their own. Young people wanted to build their own house. Indeed "WE WANT HOUSES" became a national chant.[81] As a young couple in San Francisco's Telegraph Hill and part of the artist community, they had been fascinated with the harbor—its docks, fishing boats, tugs, great ferryboats, ocean liners, and the magnificent panorama. This experience was formative and created an "urge for a view."[82] They moved to Manhattan, found an apartment on Jones Street in Greenwich Village, and began searching for rooftops with harbor views.

Their journey around the city took them to the Battery and the outer boroughs. They pushed northward, staying close to the river, and explored Westchester and the artist colony in Croton. These searches proved futile until a friend recommended the west side of the Hudson and Sneden's Landing. They took the Hudson rail line to Dobbs Ferry, walked to the river, and pulled a rope hanging on a white signboard, uncovering a black bull's-eye used to summon the ferry from across the river. As they crossed the Hudson they enjoyed their first view of the Palisades. Upon landing they made their way to Molly Sneden's tavern. This first encounter with Rockland won them over: "After the dirt and din of life in the house on Jones Street in the city, the quiet of this out of the beaten path village, was like a bit of heaven."[83]

They had a chance meeting with Mrs. Mary Lawrence Tonetti who provided directions through to Sparkill, Piermont, and Nyack and prophetically warned that "some day wide highways will be built through our country and bring the city of New York much closer."[84]

They fell in love with the village of Grand View, which reminded them of Telegraph Hill, and the Tappan Zee, almost as wide as San Francisco Bay; Tarrytown across the river was a good stand-in for the cities across the Bay, while the hills of Westchester appeared not unlike Berkeley's hills. This charming, simple village on the river was by "far the most perfect answer to our needs."[85]

While farmland prices were good, the lack of rapid transportation was a drawback to potential new home-owning commuters. However, for the Haders this was one of the great charms of the country—a restful peace and quiet every-

Undated photograph of the Bight, located along the shores of South Nyack and Grand View *John F. Geist, photographer. HSRC Collection*

where. The Haders embodied the values of the country life and rural Rockland. They felt at home in the premodern world of Grand View, which stood as a bulwark against the forces of urbanization and hurry up. They appreciated what was at stake and recognized that the "Bridge Wars" were about more than a river crossing. Rockland would be changed in fundamental ways and their sanctuary on River Road in Grand View threatened.

Now Fred Horn took to the field to meet his adversary and moved quickly to organize grassroots support. Local papers announced, HORN LEADING MOVEMENT FOR HUDSON SPAN—BEARS EXPENSE OF CIRCULATING PETITIONS IN ROCKLAND AND WESTCHESTER. His stated goal was 20,000 signatures. He ridiculed statements that the taxpayers would suffer as a result of the bridge and reported receiving many letters from Republicans and Democrats, both endorsing it. He claimed no ulterior motive except to build the bridge, which he thought "would be a great project, despite what others have been saying to condemn it . . . those he calls, the selfish few." The citizens of Rockland, according to Horn, "deserve better than to travel so far out of their way to reach Westchester . . . property values will not fall."[86] The key term here is "the selfish few," an effort to label bridge opponents as rich elitists driven by self-interest.

Horn presented the governor with a petition of 5,000 signatures and had another 4,000 names on other petitions. Letters to the editor of *The Journal-News* supported the bridge at Grand View. R. Sigerist wrote:

The Bight, along the shores of South Nyack and Grand View *HSRC Collection*

He doesn't understand the call to preserve the beauty of the landscape, when so many bridges built around the world are architectural gems, including the GWB. And as for the people who are concerned about their estates, he names the Chase Williams' place in Grand View, which has been unoccupied for 9 years and no one wants to buy it because they can't afford it. These people live in the past, time marches forward, progress is necessary. "What man at first condemns, he later on finds it a blessing in disguise."[87]

Mrs. C. Gilson of Grand View felt the protesters were wasting their time and driven by selfish motives:

They don't understand that in order to help those who need it, someone has to pay, and everyone's home is dear to them. The protesters rarely cross the Hudson, especially in winter, because if they needed to cross it often, they wouldn't be complaining. And if they were truly concerned about preserving the beauty of the river, they would do something about the crumbling piers everywhere and the foul pollution that has turned the Hudson into a sewer, unfit for even fish to swim in.[88]

Rockland–Westchester Bridge Straw Poll, 1936 *Courtesy Craig H. Long.*
Reprinted with permission: The Journal News/Gannett Co. Inc.

John Crowley summed up the argument of the advocates when he asked,

> How much longer must Rockland County remain a vest pocket used conve-
> niently only by a small minority? Every naysayer had protested such develop-
> ments as the Rockland Theatre in Haverstraw and the new school or post office
> in Nyack, and yet it is these same people and many more who cannot imagine
> not having them around. Rockland County must progress and fortunately there
> are enough progressive citizens affiliated with all the political parties to prevent
> any attempt to retard it.[89]

Crowley's call to the progressive forces is a reminder that the "Bridge Wars"
framed the question as a fundamental struggle for the future of Rockland County.
Both sides saw this moment as decisive.

A straw poll was initiated by *The Journal-News* asking, "Are You For or Against
Construction of Proposed Hudson River Bridge?" The public was urged to fill out
the printed ballot in the newspaper and mail it in. They were asked for their opinions on a logical site, effects on the communities near the Rockland approach,
impact on the rest of the county, and, if applicable, their reasons for opposing.

Tappan Zee Bay, Piermont, N. Y.

The Tappan Zee from Piermont, circa 1910 *HSRC Collection*

Over the next few weeks the poll results moved back and forth, depending on the efforts of the two groups.

Hader and Horn now went at it hand-to-hand. Horn accused Hader of unfair tactics in the straw poll, saying he'd purchased 100 copies of the newspaper and solicited opposing votes. Horn also challenged Hader's statement that Nyack officials had gone on record saying they opposed the bridge, when in fact no action had been taken. He also barbed at Hader directly: "If the bridge is built, he can no longer sit on his porch and watch the eels playing leap frog at low tide, but he can see the fish chasing crabs from the bridge."[90]

Early in October 1936, protesters rallied on board a ferry in the Tappan Zee. More than 150 indignant residents of Rockland and Westchester demanded the site be located elsewhere. William C. Osborn, President of the Hudson River Conservation Association, asked why this bridge was to be built at the three-mile point when to the south, the state owned land and the river was only a mile wide. He warned that construction of the bridge would also destroy the beauty of the Tappan Zee. Osborn urged the state legislature to create a Hudson River Commission that would have the power to preserve the beauties of the valley. Colonel Charles O. Gunther of Grand View, a mathematician, argued that from an engineer's standpoint, there was no economic reason to build a bridge there. Dr. Leslie Case of the Tarrytown Historical Society said construction of a bridge at this point was in flagrant disregard of all principles of natural conservation.[91]

Despite the negativity, Horn's supporters pulled ahead in the straw poll. Some respondents argued that "it would make Grand View of some use to the county."

One stated that "It's all right to want residential communities but what about the fellow who has to find a job and earn his living? Scenic beauty won't pay his grocery bills."[92] The class edge was becoming increasingly clear as the battle raged—elite versus everyman, artists versus common folk.

The Journal-News closed its straw vote on the proposed Hudson River bridge in late October, with 702 votes in favor of the bridge and 405 against. The strongest opposition developed in Grand View and South Nyack, Grand View casting 127 votes against the bridge to 17 for, while the South Nyack vote was 58 against to 17 for. Spring Valley and Monsey cast the largest vote for the bridge, Spring Valley voting 126 for to 7 against and Monsey voting 111 for to 1 against. The voices of progress seemed to have won the paper ballot war.[93]

It seemed fitting indeed that nature would have the last word in the "Bridge Wars." Borings at one spot off Grand View, where a foundation for the main span would have been located, went down 180 feet without striking rock or hardpan. "They'll never build a bridge for $9,000,000 at that depth," one of the engineers commented. Mrs. Mary Mowbray-Clarke, president of the Rockland County branch of the Hudson River Conservation Association, had predicted a month earlier that a deep geological rift under the Tappan Zee would doom the bridge project more surely than organized protests. Surveyors intimated that operations might be shifted elsewhere if another test or two disclosed a similar depth of hardpan.[94] Rumors circulated that borings had to reach 200 feet before striking hardpan. Hader rejoiced, reminding everyone that 100 feet was the engineers' cut-off point.

In November, Dr. Hughes of the Hudson River Crossing Authority declared no bridge would be built between Nyack and Tarrytown or, in all likelihood, anywhere along the Tappan Zee. The borings were too deep and the cost was prohibitive. Many thought the "Bridge War" was over and the forces of preservation had triumphed; in fact, it was only a truce, albeit one extended by the duration of World War II. Hader and the opponents had only been given a reprieve.

CAMP SHANKS

In the fall of 1942 Major Drew Eberson visited Orangeburg and selected over 2,000 acres for an army embarkation point; thus he brought World War II to Rockland County. Farmland was turned into a city of 50,000 people. Camp "Last Stop USA" was a transfer point for troops going abroad to fight and also processed POWs and wounded soldiers returning from the front. After the war the camp barracks were turned into apartments for 4,000 families of former GIs, most of whom were Columbia University students. Camp Shanks had become Shanks Village, the largest veteran-student housing complex in the United States.[95] Frugal lifestyles, primitive accommodations, and low rents characterized this experiment in community living. The self-contained village, sometimes referred to as a "baby factory," was a response to the chronic postwar housing shortage. In 1951 Columbia withdrew its sponsorship, and over the next five years residents left and parcels were sold to developers as well as to New York State for the Palisades Interstate Parkway.[96]

A key moment in determining the future of Camp Shanks occurred in 1946 when Republican State Assemblyman Robert Walmsley appealed to the War Department not to turn Shanks into a national cemetery, which many thought a logical suggestion given its designation as the "Last Stop." In recalling his letter to the Secretary of War, Walmsley noted that he wrote, "It would be most unwise at this time to take Shanks away from the military, and to turn it into a cemetery so close to a major metropolitan area where people were in need of housing would be inappropriate."[97]

The secretary agreed and thus enabled Walmsley's vision of a postwar Rockland suburb to survive. On a visit to Shanks, Columbia President Dwight Eisenhower commented, "With the housing shortage the way it is today, it's good to have a place where there is shade, grass and birds."[98] In a survey in May 1953, of the 1,300 families in residence, 950 stated they intended to remain in Rockland County "either because they cannot afford to go anywhere else or because they liked living here."[99] *Inside Shanks*, a booklet printed by two Shanks Villagers, noted in its conclusion that "Others have taken enough deep breaths of Rockland County air to want more of it."[100] Shanks Village served to fix Rockland's future as a suburban development, cloaked in the mantle of patriotism.

World War II left two additional legacies—one in engineering and the other in international politics—pertinent to Rockland's development. The war necessitated many technological innovations. In planning for the D-Day invasion at Normandy, engineers sank ships and large concrete boxes to form an artificial breakwater that permitted troops and supplies to be landed. This experience working with caissons would be invaluable in planning for the deep piers required for a crossing of the Hudson River.

The bombing of the Japanese cities of Hiroshima and Nagasaki ushered in the Atomic Age. The nuclear cloud that hung over the postwar world shaped the narrative of the Cold War and created a profound urban anxiety.[101] With the acceptance of civilian bombing as a way to break the enemy's morale and will to fight, the war left an indelible mark on the nuclear discourse of the 1950s.[102] The atomic bomb altered the meaning of distance, and it became impossible to separate the dangers of the bomb from the dangers of the city. Urban centers like New York were vulnerable targets with indefensible concentrations of population. The centrifugal forces of population dispersion were now energized by the twin demons of urban decay and the nuclear threat. As cities increasingly looked like unnatural places, flight seemed a valid response. The ubiquitous diagrams of the concentric circles of nuclear destruction from Hiroshima now became exit maps for anxious urbanites.[103] The automobile and the new highways provided the means and the pathway to the new citadel—the American suburb, where the family would serve as the center of normal life amid the threat of nuclear destruction.

New York City seemed to be in the crosshairs of the Soviets' nuclear sights. These anxieties fed the calls for spatial dispersion, industrial and infrastructure decentralization, highway construction, and a general encouragement of suburbanization.[104] *The New York Times* reported on a rural and suburban realty boom instigated by bomb fears.[105] President Eisenhower warned that "in case of atomic attack on our key cities (read New York), the road must permit quick evacuation of the target areas." Unsurprisingly, 85 percent of the new houses built between 1948 and 1958 were in the suburbs.[106]

This atomic shadow was brought closer to home when the "big golf ball," a radar installation that was part of a Nike missile defense project, was installed on a hill in Orangeburg. It remained operational from 1955 to 1974, ready to warn New York City from the relative safety of Rockland County.[107]

The central importance of automobiles to suburban development is taken as an article of faith. This is documented in the connection between automobile use and population density. In 1922, approximately 135,000 homes in 60 cities had become dependent on automobile transportation. By 1940, 13 million homes did not have access to public transportation. As dependence on the automobile increased, population densities fell. In 1920, the average density of urbanized areas (cities, suburbs, and towns) in the United States was 6,160 people per square mile; in 1990 that figure was only 2,589. In fact, the average density of developments built since 1960 was only 1,469 people per square mile. The motor vehicle, as one critic stated, "has a voracious appetite for land."[108]

The focus on the automobile is complemented by the major impact of the expressway in directing suburban development. Highway engineers, who came to dominate the planning and construction of state highways in the 1930s and 1940s, shared ideas with their European counterparts. They found in the Autobahn in Germany a powerful model of the highway of the future. First constructed in the

1920s, this limited-access, high-speed, landscaped expressway controlled three critical domains—territory, speed, and communications.[109] The Autobahn and its accompanying map production served to shrink distance, unify political geographies, and promote travel as part of a new automobile-oriented society.[110] One historian has labeled the highway the preeminent "centrifugal space" of the twentieth century.[111]

Autobahn engineers and administrators took special pride in the bridges that "enabled all the structures to fit together as individual links in a chain."[112] These imposing bridges, many of them using classical design vocabularies, expressed the monumentality of the project and its powerful unifying attributes. They were the most compelling metaphor for the Autobahn.[113]

Many of the ideas about the modern, fluid expressway not only made their way into American culture from professional conversations among engineers but also were fixed in the public consciousness by the 1939 New York World's Fair and the General Motors Pavilion's "Futurama." Developed by Norman Bel Geddes, the industrial designer and advocate of streamlined design, who published *Magic Motorways* in 1940, "Futurama" was the most popular exhibit. Bel Geddes explored the potentialities of streamlining and speed in the 1930s and targeted the decaying, outmoded highway system.[114] His vision of a rationalized, magnificent transcontinental highway network, with lanes for speeds up to 100 miles per hour, captivated the public, who came in droves to the exhibit and left enthralled.[115]

In *Magic Motorways*, Bel Geddes, whose photographs of highway models depicted an immaculate system of predominantly eight-lane motorways, wrote,

> Motorways . . . will overpass and underpass each other, using wide-flowing developments of present-day cloverleafs; their traffic streams in the opposite direction will be completely separated, and individual lanes in the same direction will be segregated by separators. Although on the map they look like solid lines shooting across the country, actually they are complicated mechanisms which differentiate sharply between through and maneuvering traffic, and which provide automatically safe means for entering and leaving the motorways. Their lanes are designed for three separate and constant speeds of 50, 75, and 100 miles an hour. Their grades are constant, never excessive. Their curving radii are constant, always generous. All over the United States, the motorways are uniform and function in exactly the same way.[116]

This kind of thinking influenced the imaginations of the New York State engineers, planners, and politicians as they began to conceptualize a "thruway" to modernize the state's long-neglected highways.

Highway construction in the 1930s was increasingly dominated by engineers and traffic planners, whose expertise was based on scientific rationality and transcended narrow local interests and corrupt politicians. During the depression, highway construction, often funded by PWA monies, served to create jobs and modernize roads. One of the key effects of this program was to continue the process of bureaucratization and centralization, which eroded local power and control of right-of-way. Local governments and the public became increasingly comfortable with this arrangement.[117]

Governor Thomas E. Dewey, recognizing the need for road modernization and a superhighway to integrate and connect diverse regions of the state, and flush with a wartime highway fund surplus and fresh memories of "Futurama," proposed a 535-mile "Mainline for the Empire State." By 1942, outlines of the New York State Thruway appeared on official maps. The proposed 200-foot-wide self-liquidating toll road, with a center mall and limited access, would extend 486 miles from New York City to Buffalo, bypassing cities in between.

The thruway thus borrowed from earlier rural and suburban parkways the limited access that effectively prevented slow-moving vehicles from entering and exiting moving traffic, thus reducing collision risk and allowing higher traffic speeds. Grade separation allowed continuous movement, thereby effectively doubling road capacity, reducing crossing routes, and nearly eliminating the possibility of accidents. The promise in these engineering principles was greater traffic volumes at higher speeds with fewer collisions.[118]

Dewey saw highways as "the vital arteries of economic and social life."[119] In 1945 the governor's budget message noted that during the depression years, traffic and congestion steadily increased while time and use took their toll on the roads. Highway development failed to keep pace with traffic volume and wear. A substantial reconstruction program was needed, and, in addition, Dewey reiterated the need for the development of a through-way, or express motorway, to bind the state together from New York City to Buffalo. He estimated it would cost $640 million and would require federal aid, approximately $110 million.[120]

Bertram D. Tallamy, Deputy State Superintendent of Public Works and a key figure in the thruway construction, predicted that with its promise of seven-hour runs across New York, it would enrich the state. Speed was now closely linked to economic growth and communal networking.[121]

In December, the state announced that the new thruway, referred to as the Catskill Thruway, would have a Suffern terminus, and Route 17 traffic woes would end. It would pass through Harriman and Central Valley, angle toward the Hudson, and end west of Albany at McKownsville. Traffic from New York City would go over the George Washington Bridge and pass through northern New Jersey on Routes 4 and 202, and these four-lane arteries would be widened to conform to New York's thruway pattern. When the Palisades Interstate Parkway was completed, that route would be available to pick up the thruway as well. These early plans included no new Hudson crossing, given the expectation of linking with New Jersey's highway system.[122]

The portion of the thruway to be constructed across Rockland County would become not only a major new thoroughfare but also a most important gateway for vehicular traffic moving to and from the New York City area. Rockland topography contained some of the most difficult engineering challenges in the highway's 486-mile length. The Ramapo Pass is the only water-level opening in the Ramapo Mountains, and the valley was narrow and already occupied by the Ramapo River, Route 17, and the Erie Railroad. The thruway had grade standards of no more than 3 percent and no curves less than a half-mile in radius, so the road could not be carried over the mountains. The grade issue was key to maintaining speed and traffic flow, especially for trucks.

Work began on the New York State Thruway on July 11, 1946, when Dewey broke ground at a point near Liverpool, a few miles northwest of Syracuse. Completion was expected in 1951, but within a year an extended delay was announced; rumors that the project would be abandoned were rampant. Dewey's ambitious timetable was jeopardized in 1947 by a shortage of materials, especially steel, with its fluctuating prices and uncertain delivery dates. As a result, certain jobs did not go out for bids. It was the same with lumber. In general, major structures were deleted from the 1946 program, with operations limited to work on the rights-of-way between the sites and between bridges and other major structures.[123]

Charles H. Sells, Superintendent of Public Works, stated the reasons for the delay and reassured the public that, "this is Governor Dewey's pet project . . . no other state in the nation and no other country in the world will have a highway like this, and I am proud to have had a hand in originating it. What the Erie Canal was to the early development of this state, the super-highway will be to the development of automobile traffic of the future, especially commercial traffic."[124] Dewey's determination and the analogy to the Erie Canal placed the thruway on a historic continuum with other transportation innovations.

In February 1950, in response to the pressure to move ahead, Dewey appointed a special committee to consider a revised scheme for making the proposed $400 million thruway self-liquidating by a variation of the toll system. And most critically for Rockland, instead of terminating at the New Jersey–Rockland border on the west bank of the Hudson, the superhighway would cross the Hudson somewhere between Peekskill and Yonkers and continue down the east shore of the river to connect with the Major Deegan Expressway or some other arterial route. For Rocklanders like former Assemblyman Ferdinand R. Horn, now president of the Rockland County Chapter of the New York Good Roads Association, the fifteen-year-old dream seemed nearer to a reality: the State of New York recognized it needed a Hudson crossing for its thruway. This was a result of the lack of agreement with New Jersey on a suitable exit from New York State through New Jersey to New York City.[125]

It was a decisive moment in Rockland's history when the Hudson River crossing was resuscitated and embodied in the thruway proposals. For those opposed to the bridge, the thruway seemed a kind of Trojan horse, concealing the Tappan Zee Bridge within. It would become increasingly difficult for local citizens to tease out the bridge questions from the more dominant and immediate thruway issues of right-of-way. Whether by design or by chance, folding the two issues into one distracted the public and bifurcated the opposition. So many things to watch for, so many questions to ask, and so many voices to be heard dissipated public energy and fragmented the response. The context for the 1950s debate was far more diffuse than the struggles of the 1930s. *The Journal-News* fully understood the difference: "14 years ago, it was a matter of building a bridge—not a bridge and Thruway, which is an entirely different matter."[126]

In April 1950, in an effort to insulate the project from political haggling and local self-interest, Dewey proposed a Thruway Authority, a public authority to finance, construct, and maintain the road. This ensconced the engineers and the traffic experts and sanctified the planning, giving the project a preeminent legitimacy and making it difficult for the affected villages, towns, and cities to dispute decisions made in the name of the public interest. The ensuing four years of debate seem in retrospect a David and Goliath battle in which the state used the weight and expertise of the authority to blunt opponents and quiet critics.

The announcement of the Hudson River crossing between Peekskill and Yonkers stirred local officials, boards of supervisors, and organized community groups to ask for maps of the project. Where would the bridge cross and what was the exact route of the thruway through Rockland? The standard evasive response to both questions was "the route depended on the engineering studies," "the engineering studies," "the studies."

Bertram D. Tallamy, now Chairman of the New York State Thruway Authority, announced that preliminary engineering investigations would begin so that the thruway could enter the New York metropolitan area through Westchester, necessitating the construction of a bridge across the river as part of the route. State engineers visited Grand View's waterfront, checking the area with a map of the

proposed Horn bridge from 1937. Test borings were made 200 feet out from Salisbury Point to determine at what depth bedrock would be found. The presence of
the engineers' barge filled the village with a sense of *déjà vu*.

Grand View erupted. Residents protested that the ghost of the bridge had returned to haunt them. As in 1936, many of the same players and sentiments appeared. Elmer Hader was again determined to fight the bridge with any means
possible, still insisting views would be spoiled. The mayor, Francis McGoldrick,
remarked that he thought the construction of the bridge was impractical. The
argument continued about having the bridge go through Haverstraw or Nyack
instead.[127]

More groups announced their opposition. South Nyack families feared the
span would mar the beauty of the Tappan Zee and feared for their fine homes;
Salisbury Point residents worried about their view. Instead of preserving the beauty, residents predicted, the bridge would lead to pollution and traffic. Sailboating
was mentioned as another popular pastime that could go by the wayside.[128]

In May a meeting of 150 residents from Grand View, Sneden's Landing, and
South Nyack formed a committee against the bridge, but it lacked the fire of past
meetings. A petition only had a few signatures on it, but efforts were under way
to bring the number up to 20,000. Elmer Hader and his wife were absent and left
a letter to be read, urging, "Do not be lulled into inaction." It seemed even the
Haders had lost their energy.[129]

The Port Authority finally acknowledged the bridge would be placed in the
Grand View area, outside its jurisdiction. Dewey categorically affirmed that only
one bridge would be built and that the Thruway Authority would build it. The
location would be as near the Nyack/Tarrytown area as conditions permitted.
He reiterated the benefits of the bridge in solving New York City's arterial traffic
problem, enabling motorists to drive to the Catskills from Brooklyn in less than
two hours and avoid all the horrible traffic jams on the west side of the Hudson.
And most astonishingly, he concluded, "If I were in the real estate business, I'd
plunge on buying land in Rockland County."[130]

New counterproposals abounded, including one from the Citizens Budget
Committee to dam the Hudson River, to provide freshwater for New York City
and a thruway bridge for Westchester and Rockland. The dam, which would
prevent salt water from mixing with freshwater, would have locks for shipping
and make the upper Hudson more navigable by raising the water level. The dam/
bridge would be placed north of Haverstraw. What inspired such a proposal? The
area was experiencing a drought.[131]

C. Earle Morrow, a member of the New York Regional Plan Association, called
for more of a public voice in planning the future development of Rockland Coun-

ty. He warned that only action by responsible citizens would secure strict zoning and building codes.[132] A newspaper editorial complained that many areas of Rockland did not have zoning laws in place and now, in the face of the thruway, were scrambling to get such laws on the books. Speculators were buying land at an unprecedented rate. The thruway would most likely come through areas that were topographically accessible, and those needed protection. Municipalities would be wise to start the zoning process immediately.[133]

Dewey now played the defense card, cautioning the public that because of the "grim recent events in Korea," it was more important than ever to have a road like the thruway to move armaments and troops rapidly for deployment where needed. He maintained that it was the business of government to be prepared: "if anyone ever does drop a bomb on New York City, you won't hear any more arguments about whether New York City needs the Thruway."[134] At a 1951 hearing conducted by the U.S. Army Corps of Engineers in New York City, Robert Moses, speaking for the City of New York and the State Park Authority, stated that the Tappan Zee Bridge would be an important link in connecting roads for national defense.[135]

Finally in August 1950 the state announced that the thruway would enter Rockland at Sloatsburg, east of the Ramapo River, and cross Route 202 north of the village of Suffern, intersecting Route 59 in the vicinity of Airmont and Route 45, south of the Nyack Turnpike in Spring Valley. It would then pass over Route 304 between Pearl River and Nanuet and cross Route 303 south of West Nyack, about halfway to Orangeburg. It would continue over Route 9W below South Nyack, connecting with a bridge at the north end of Grand View. The route could still be changed and the exact location of the bridge was still under study.[136] In December a decision was reached for a crossing of the Hudson River from just below Salisbury Point, south of Route 59, on the west bank to the south end of Tarrytown opposite Route 119, where it joins Route 9 on the east bank.

Reactions to the thruway plan and the bridge placement ranged from frustration in Grand View to favorable responses throughout the rest of the county. Most agreed that December's announced plan, in which the road was to run north of Route 59 and through the middle of the county, was more logical than a line south of Route 59. Although residents of Nyack and the surrounding area were determined to fight, the general mood was one of acceptance.[137]

Thruway Authority Chairman Tallamy defended the plan to span the Hudson at the widest point and stated that the route through Rockland was in relation to the entire project and "the alignment must be on the basis of maximum utility and service to all potential users, and only by keeping in mind the basic purposes of the project as an express artery, and by placing the general public inter-

ɔo Valley Independent

ɔr neighbors in Airmont, Hillburn, Ladentown, Mahwah, Monsey, Pomona, Ramapo, Sloatsburg, Southfields, Suffern, Tallman, Tuxedo and Viola.

Suffern, N. Y., Thursday, January 17, 1952   Member New York Press Ass'n   Member National Editorial Ass'n   Ten Cents

Thruway To Go South Of Rt. 59, Wipe Out 60 Homes In Suffern

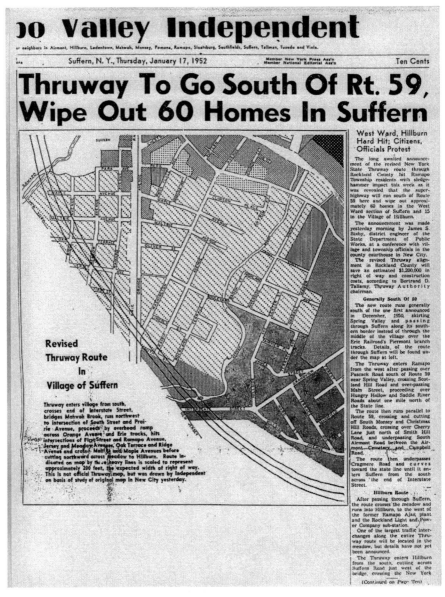

Revised Thruway Route In Village of Suffern

Thruway enters village from south, crosses end of Interstate Street, bridges Mahwah Brook, runs northwest to intersection of South Street and Prairie Avenue, proceeds by overhead ramp across Orange Avenue and Erie tracks, hits intersections of First Street and Ramapo Avenue, Jersey and Meadow Avenues, Oak Terrace and Ridge Avenue and cross Maltbie and Maple Avenues before cutting northward across meadow to Hillburn. Route indicated on map by the heavy lines is scaled to represent approximately 200 feet, the expected width of right of way. This is not official Thruway map, but was drawn by Independent on basis of study of original map in New City yesterday.

West Ward, Hillburn Hard Hit; Citizens, Officials Protest

The long awaited announcement of the revised New York State Thruway route through Rockland County hit Ramapo Township residents with sledgehammer impact this week as it was revealed that the superhighway will run south of Route 59 here and wipe out approximately 60 homes in the West Ward section of Suffern and 15 in the Village of Hillburn.

The announcement was made yesterday morning by James S. Bixby, district engineer of the State Department of Public Works, at a conference with village and township officials in the county courthouse in New City.

The revised Thruway alignment in Rockland County will save an estimated $1,200,000 in right of way and construction costs, according to Bertrand D. Tallamy, Thruway Authority chairman.

Generally South Of 59

The new route runs generally south of the one first announced in December, 1950, skirting Spring Valley and passing through Suffern along its southern border instead of through the middle of the village over the Erie Railroad's Piermont branch tracks. Details of the route through Suffern will be found under the map at left.

The Thruway enters Ramapo from the west after passing over Pascack Road south of Route 59 near Spring Valley, crossing Scotland Hill Road and over-passing Main Street, proceeding over Hungry Hollow and Saddle River Roads about one mile north of the State line.

The route then runs parallel to Route 59, crossing and cutting off South Monsey and Christmas Hill Roads, crossing over Cherry Lane just north of Smith Hill Road, and underpassing South Airmont Road between the Airmont Cemetery and Campbell Road.

The route then underpasses Cragmere Road and curves toward the state line until it enters Suffern from the south across the end of Interstate Street.

Hillburn Route

After passing through Suffern, the route crosses the meadow and runs into Hillburn, to the west of the former Ramapo Ajax plant and the Rockland Light and Power Company sub-station.

One of the largest traffic interchanges along the entire Thruway route will be located in the meadow, but details have not yet been announced.

The Thruway enters Hillburn from the south, cutting across Suffern Road just west of the bridge, crossing the New York

(Continued on Page Ten)

Article from the *Ramapo Valley Independent,* detailing the possible destruction of Suffern by the thruway   *Courtesy Craig H. Long*

Thruway Route Shift Puts Road South of
Turnpike From Suffern West Ward to Nanuet

NEW YORK STATE THRUWAY AUTHORITY

Pictured in the proposed new route of the New York State Thruway, originally planned to run north of Route 59 all the way from Suffern to Nyack. The Thruway route is shown in the broken line, the parkway, which it crosses at Bardonia, by the dotted line. The outlined areas are unincorporated villages.

Map showing one of many changes in the New York State Thruway plan   *Courtesy Craig H. Long.*
Reprinted with permission: The Journal News/*Gannett Co. Inc.*

ests above local interest can the over all objectives be achieved." Local conditions could not govern the choice of the thruway route. The bridge location decision had to be economically based because it would be in a position to serve multiple lanes of traffic.[138]

The key words in Tallamy's comments were "utility," "service," and "users." But for whom were these services to be offered? Who would be the users? Certainly not the locals. The answer seems to have been the "consumer-motorist," whose gasoline taxes and other user fees fed the highway machine and made Tallamy beholden to automobile owners, the industry, and the lobbyists.[139]

Thruway planners recognized that something fundamental had changed. In an address to the Westchester County Association, Tallamy commented, "Passenger vehicles are no longer luxuries. They move people to and from their work. The almost universal ownership of cars has fostered mushrooming suburbia far removed from industrial centers. . . . In brief our whole economy has become

Poster printed by Rockland County Committee for the Tappan Zee Bridge, January 1951.
Notice Ferdinand Horn is temporary president of the group. *Courtesy Craig H. Long. Reprinted with permission: The Journal News/Gannett Co. Inc.*

dependent on the motor vehicle and the highways over which it rolls."[140]

In May 1953 he reminded a group of *Westchester Business Magazine* editors that highways were "the molders of your community, for that is the actual fact. . . . The highways in your community have shaped and will shape the whole pattern of growth." The Tappan Zee Bridge in particular, he noted, "will make neighbors of the thousands of people who rebel against leaving their backyards to shop."[141] Tallamy concluded that "the American way of life is irrevocably geared to the motor vehicle."[142]

Thruway planners and engineers believed the country had changed in fundamental ways affecting not only residential life but also, more critically, the very pulse of economic development. Postwar anxiety about economic recovery was a key concern for public officials and thus central to discussions about the impact of the thruway. This in part explains state officials' sense of urgency in pressing for fast completion. Economic recovery and prosperity depended on it. It was no surprise when in January 1951, over solid Democratic opposition, the State Assembly approved a proposed amendment to the Constitution to place the state's credit behind $300 million in bonds for the thruway.[143]

While controversy swirled around the right-of-way, the details of the thruway's exact location were closely guarded by the authority. Indeed, the staged approach to the construction fragmented the opposition and reduced their reaction time by revealing plans only late in the day. One of the principal battlegrounds was Suffern, where in 1953 the village attempted to halt the thruway work near the village wells. Attorney William Sichol said that villagers were angry about plans to divert the Ramapo River directly over the wells. The trustees feared the work might damage and pollute their water supply. Suffern wanted a guarantee that water purity would be maintained and issued an injunction against further work.[144]

Village police physically ejected six New York State Thruway workers from the town's waterworks site on November 11, threatening to shoot them if they dared try again to set up a drill near the village wells. Village Trustee John C. Petrone confronted them and ordered the drillers to leave; when they refused, the police escorted them off the property.[145] Suffern took the thruway to court and eventually settled the matter, thereby protecting the village's water.

The Suffern battle was a sign of how provoked a community could become in the face of what they perceived as an overbearing, autocratic authority. These events contributed to the sense of powerlessness that alarmed locals and fueled more open opposition to highway projects in the late 1950s and '60s.

Nothing added to the sense of helplessness more than the displacement of homes and local businesses. Newspaper stories were often accompanied by vivid photographs of historic buildings being razed, homes being moved, and streets

napo Valley Independent

ing the news of your neighbors in Airmont, Hillburn, Ladentown, Mahwah, Monsey, Ramapo, Sloatsburg, Southfields, Suffern, Tallman, Tuxedo and Viola.

Member of Audit Bureau of Circulations

Suffern, N. Y., Thursday, January 24, 1952.

Member New York Press Ass'n Member National Editorial Ass'n

Ten Cents

Hillburn Mayor Proposes New Thruway Route Over Mountain

State To Study Plan By-Passing Hillburn, Suffern, Sloatsburg

State Thruway officials agreed on Monday to make an engineering and cost study of an alternate Thruway route which would cross the Ramapo Mountains north of here and completely avoid the villages of Suffern, Hillburn and Sloatsburg.

The alternate plan was drawn up by Mayor Charles R. Banker of Hillburn and presented to State officials at a conference held Monday afternoon in the Hillburn firehouse.

James S. Bixby, district engineer of the State Department of Public Works from Poughkeepsie, told Mayor Banker and other Hillburn officials that they were entitled to an honest, detailed study of the proposal, and that it would be started immediately.

Mayor Banker's plan, illustrated in the map at left, has the Thruway departing from the State route south of Monsey, and proceeding north-west across the Erie Piermont branch and Route 59 between Monsey and Tallman.

Mayor Banker's Route

It continues north-west until it crosses Viola Road between Mile and Spook Rock Roads, then curves across Route 202 and runs south-west alongside the mountain until it reaches a point north of the Suffern village line.

The route then curves up and over the mountain in a northwesterly direction and descends to a proposed interchange in the Torne Valley, running parallel but to the east of the State route until it hits Orange County.

Mayor Banker stated that his route met the Thruway specifications in that it involved no grade over 3 percent and that the turns were based on a radius of over 3,000 feet.

He also pointed out that his route does not cross either the Erie Railroad, Route 17 or the Ramapo River, is the same length as the State route, misses Hillburn and Sloatsburg completely, and passes through mountainous land of little value.

Ideal Bomb Target

The State route crosses the Erie Railroad, Route 17 and the Ramapo River twice, he said, destroys 60 to 75 homes in Suffern, 15 to 20 homes in Hillburn, pierces the interchange on low swampy ground, and makes the Ramapo Gap an ideal bombing target.

At the conference with Hillburn officials, and later at the evening conference with the Suffern Board of Trustees, Mr. Bixby and five other Thruway engineers pointed out a number of objections to Mayor Banker's plan.

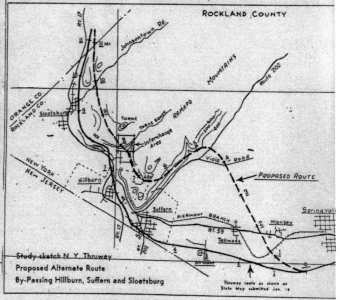

ROCKLAND COUNTY

RT. 0

Johnsontown Rd.

MOUNTAINS

Route 202

ORANGE CO. ROCKLAND CO.

Sloatsburg

TORNE

TORNE BROOK

RAMAPO

Interchange Area

Viola & Road

PROPOSED ROUTE

NEW YORK NEW JERSEY

Hillburn

Suffern

PIERMONT BRANCH

Spring Vall

Monsey

RT. 59

Tallman

Airmont

Study sketch N. Y. Thruway
Proposed Alternate Route
By-Passing Hillburn, Suffern and Sloatsburg

Thruway route as shown on State Map submitted Jan. 16

Mr. Bixby told both groups that he thought the Hillburn proposal involved difficulties that could not be overcome, that it was doubtful that it would be adopted, but that it was entitled to a thorough study.

"Nothing would make me happier than to get the Thruway outside of Suffern and Hillburn," he said.

Objection To Alternate

Among the objections which Mr. Bixby and his associates saw in the Banker route were too sharp a rise and fall in the route over the mountain. He said that an attempt was being made to keep the route as near to the water-level route of the Erie as possible so that trucks could operate on it economically.

The mountain crossing also involves ice and snow difficulties in wintertime, he said. Mayor Banker's plan involved taking the roadway 600 feet high, which Thruway engineers are trying to avoid wherever possible. They

Banker Route

(Continued from Page One)

are keeping the route generally under 600 feet elevation, he said.

Edward B. Shrope, chief Thruway engineer, also pointed out that the location of the interchange was of major importance since it was expected that 40,000 cars per day would pass through it.

The interchange will require 35 acres of level land, he said, and should be located as near as possible to Routes 202 and 17 so that it would be readily accessible to New Jersey traffic.

In Mr. Bixby's party were Edward B. Shrope, chief Thruway engineer; Conrad H. Lang, deputy Thruway engineer; Newton F. Renan, assistant State engineer for Rockland County; Elmer Carlson, chief planning engineer at Poughkeepsie, and William L'Estrange, his assistant.

Present at the Hillburn meeting were Trustees William S. Hane and Fred R. Henion, Clerk James J. Eathorne, and James Mulligan, J. Edgar Davidson and Franklin W. Eacher.

At the Suffern conference were Mayor Roy Spicer, Trustees Willis Clark, John Stewart, Phillip Frachman and Robert Rew, Clerk George Cox, and about a dozen spectators.

Mayor Says Send Protests To Albany

Suffern Mayor Roy E. Spicer urged this week that letters and telegrams protesting the routing of the Thruway through Suffern and Hillburn be sent to the following:

Governor Thomas E. Dewey Executive Mansion Albany, N. Y.

State Assemblyman

(Continued on Page Ten)

Article from the *Ramapo Valley Independent,* suggesting a new path for the thruway, in Hillburn *Courtesy Craig H. Long*

Valley Independent

...nent, Hillburn, Ladentown, Mahwah, Monsey, Pomona, Ramapo, Sloatsburg, Southfields, Suffern, Tallman, Tuxedo and Viola.

Suffern, N.Y., Thursday, April 10, 1952   Member New York Press Ass'n / Member National Editorial Ass'n   Ten Cents

Thruway To Run North Of Rt. 59 In Suffern; Hillburn Suffers Most

Authority Chairman Says New Route Final; West Ward Saved

A Thruway route described as the final alignment in Ramapo Township was announced yesterday by B. D. Tallamy, Thruway Authority chairman. Mr. Tallamy submitted a general map of the route at a conference with Charles W. Hawkins, Rockland County Republican Committee chairman, and Ramapo Supervisor Pincus Margulies.

The new alignment varies considerably from any of those titles far proposed, except in Hillburn where it is virtually the same as the alignment on the "West Ward route." Suffern's West Ward is avoided, as are the village's water wells and sewage plant.

From a point east of Monsey, the route is unchanged. Westerly from Monsey the Thruway will run as follows: Crosses Route 59 from south to north east of Almshouse Road; bisects Spook Rock Road about an eighth-of-a-mile north of the Tallman light; crosses Airmont Road just north of the Piermont tracks of the Erie Railroad; crosses Hemion Road about a half-mile north of Route 59, and enters Suffern at its northeasterly tip.

Crosses Over Lake

The Thruway will then cut through the northern extreme of the Suffern Stone Company quarry and pass over Lake Antrim at about the middle of the lake. The general map released by Mr. Tallamy shows the Thruway passing just north of the bathing beach and crossing Wayne Avenue near its intersection with Washington Avenue.

The alignment then takes the super-highway through the mountain behind Wayne Avenue. It will come out of the mountain and cross Route 59 again just south of the village limits.

NEW YORK STATE THRUWAY

As the Thruway leaves Suffern, it crosses the Ramapo River and proceeds through Hillburn paralleling the river on the west. The alignment through Hillburn and Ramapo appears virtually unchanged from the "West Ward route," which was proposed by the Thruway in January. Details on the number of buildings which will be destroyed by the new route were not available.

Only Minor Variations

This new route is now subject only to minor variations that may arise in the development of detail plans, Mr. Tallamy said. He added that while many variations were considered in recent route studies, the basic alignments were:

(1) The route previously preferred by the Thruway Authority, which ran through Suffern's West Ward. This involved the removal of more than 65 dwellings in Suffern.

(2) A line suggested by Mayor Charles Banker of Hillburn, which would carry the Thruway north over the Ramapo Mountains, avoiding Suffern and Hillburn entirely.

(3) A route approaching Suffern at the northerly end, avoiding the extensive property damage of the first line. This route was the one chosen.

Banker Route Out

The route proposed by Mayor Banker was ruled out on both economic and engineering grounds, according to Mr. Tallamy. Studies showed that it would cost at least four million dollars more than either of the other basic routes under consideration. He estimated that the route announced yesterday would cost three million dollars more than the West Ward alignment. It will, however, be somewhat shorter.

Referring to the Banker route, Mr. Tallamy said, "Even though it is physically possible to traverse these mountains, to do so would result in 10 miles of three per cent grade in its 14.7 mile length.

"This would not be sound engineering. This route would be potentially dangerous. Furthermore, the grades would increase operation cost, thereby diminishing the advantage of the Thruway as a commercial route."

"When economy was weighed against the rather serious disruption of a Suffern residential section, however, it was determined to seek an alternate route." Mr. Tallamy asserted. "The line finally selected not only answers many of the local objections, but ...tors can be demonstrated graphically by our traffic study. By 1960, these studies show, more than 3,500,000 vehicles will be using this section of the Thruway annually."

Mr. Tallamy said that some construction will be begun in Rockland County this fall and completion of the route is anticipated by 1954.

Commenting on the new alignment, William R. Sichol, chairman of the local Citizens Thruway Committee, said, "We are gratified that the utilities of the Village of Suffern, its sewer system and water wells, and the Athletic Field are being avoided, but to the extent that the route runs within the village limits, we are not and can not be pleased.

"From the very beginning, we have been opposed to the Thruway coming through any part of the villages of Suffern and Hillburn. Our position is unchanged.

"Though far from satisfied with the present route, the Citizens Committee is not unmindful of the fact that the new route is far less destructive to Suffern than the old 'West Ward route' or the Madigan-Hyland route."

Mr. Sichol said there will be a committee meeting to chart possible future action at the Municipal Building tomorrow at 8 p.m.

Map from the *Ramapo Valley Independent*, showing thruway route in Suffern   *Courtesy Craig H. Long*

Photograph of Doris and Irving Rion moving their home from the path of the thruway *Courtesy Doris and Irving Rion*

and old roads being uprooted. While the stories and the images were poignant, they were countered by the attitude that this was the price for progress and the public should embrace the chance for a new beginning. Much debate centered on the exact number of homes taken—more than one hundred—and the prices paid to the displaced families and owners.

In the first phase of the "Bridge Wars" in the 1930s, the crossing had been the creature of local Rockland politicians and businessmen eager to link their county with Westchester. In the second phase, the bridge was the linchpin for New York State's thruway plans to link Buffalo to New York City. The Tappan Zee Bridge moved from a bottom-up proposal initiated by local communities to a top-down plan driven by an agency of the state. These differing angles of vision partly explain the modest, if not minimal opposition and the speed with which the bridge was completed—less than four years in spite of materials shortages. The second bridge war was more of a skirmish between unequal forces in which the outcome seemed almost predetermined. Indeed, both the descriptions and the depictions of the proposed bridge moved from the monumental to the functional; from a work that stood alone as an ambitious crossing to one linked to a master roadway connecting one region of the state to another.

Most representations of the proposed bridge produced a typical iconic suspension design in imitation of the Brooklyn Bridge; by the 1930s the George Washington Bridge was the favored model. This created a double expectation, first that the bridge would embody a spectacular design that would add to, not detract from, the beauty of the river as the critics had warned, and second, that it would require a span of unprecedented scale. When the George Washington opened in 1931, the length of the bridge was 4,760 feet. The projected length of the Tappan Zee Bridge was more than 15,000 feet, including the approaches. No wonder the opposition thought it was not feasible.

The problem of the distance the bridge had to span was exacerbated by the depth of the Hudson's bedrock. The 1936 borings had not reached the pan at 100 feet, and without a solid bottom, supporting a bridge of such length seemed problematic. The issue was resolved by the work of Emil H. Praeger, former U.S. Navy Captain, who served as chief engineer for Madigan-Hyland, the consulting engineers for the Tappan Zee. During World War II, Praeger had designed rectangular buoyant concrete caissons, which were constructed in England and floated across the English Channel to form a protected harbor for the invasion of Normandy. Now, a decade later, Praeger would apply this innovative technology to the design of the Tappan Zee Bridge and use caissons to support a cantilever bridge of great expanse. These buoyant underwater foundations saved millions of dollars.

Madigan-Hyland chose to construct a cantilever bridge because this structure would reduce the stress on the girders and trusses and permit longer spans, and would withstand different rates of foundation settlement. The cantilever is a horizontal arm that extends outward with support from only one end and connects to another span. The engineering companies contracted by the Thruway Authority had experience building such bridges.[146] U.S. Steel described it as "a three mile highway in the air."[147]

The early design proposal called for an 1,112-foot steel tied-arch span bridge. One can only speculate on the aesthetic differences between the arch and the cantilever, as they would come to dominate such a prominent Hudson River vista. But finances won out, and when no bids from the fabricators were forthcoming for the arch design, engineers selected the more economical cantilever. On March 16, 1952 construction of the bridge began; it was completed on December 15, 1955. The total cost would be $60 million.

In order to experience the construction of the bridge, imagine crossing the Tappan Zee and observing structural elements as they are encountered. The traveler leaves from Nyack in Rockland County on the west shore, first passing

Falsework floating away from the bridge *HSRC Collection*

over a large reinforced concrete abutment in Grand View where the Tappan Zee Bridge connects with the land. As the car swings out onto a causeway, a six-lane concrete-deck roadway with 10-foot center mall, the road turns to the south. The 8,000-foot causeway is supported by concrete piers, spaced 50 feet apart in the river and resting on untreated timber pilings. The driver still feels he or she is on the thruway, creating the sensation of the bridge as an extension of the highway over water.

The roadway gently curves to the east and brings the driver back into a direct line for the bridge approach. A slow ascent begins; grades are restricted to three degrees. The traveler now ascends the second section of the approach, known as the west deck truss. A truss is a number of steel triangles joined together to provide increased structural strength. The west deck trusses are made of 250-foot spans supported on tall concrete piers that rest either on circular cofferdam foundations or, in the case of four west side piers, on buoyant foundations. There were a total of 19 deck truss spans, each weighing 900 tons. They were assembled at Grassy Point, 10 miles north of the bridge, on falsework, the structural skeleton that was reconfigured to meet the different heights of each truss. Railroad barges transported the falsework with a section of the deck truss perched on top. At high tide tugs hauled the falsework and the truss to the bridge site, and with the aid of the river's ebb tide and hydraulic jacks, lowered the truss onto the bridge piers with such accuracy that not one of the 14,000 anchor bolts had to be moved.

AMERICAN BRIDGE DIVISION, U. S. STEEL CORP.
PROGRESS PICTURE
General view at Tarrytown side looking
Northwest showing progress of deck
concrete on approach spans.
TAPPAN ZEE BRIDGE
DATE-Sept.2, 1955
Photographer-L.F. Stockmeyer, Nyack, N. Y.

Deck construction *HSRC Collection*

AMERICAN BRIDGE DIVISION, U. S. STEEL CORP.
PROGRESS PICTURE
View of West half of Main Cantilever
Looking Northwest from Bents 173 & 175
TAPPAN ZEE BRIDGE
DATE-Sept.16,1955
Photographer-L.F. Stockmeyer, Nyack, N. Y.

Cantilever construction *HSRC Collection*

Aerial photograph, over east side of bridge *HSRC Collection*

The driver continues the slow eastward ascent to the first section of the canti-lever bridge supported by the first tower. This 602-foot section, called the anchor arm, is a kind of steel diving board that serves to counterbalance the cantilever arm and the suspended span, which together constitute the main span. The Tap-pan Zee Bridge's main span measures 1,212 feet.

The four main towers or piers, 293 feet high, support the main span. Derricks were used to erect them. Four large, buoyant caissons provide uplift beneath the towers to reduce the loads on the steel piles below, which extend more than 280 feet down to bedrock. The caissons were also built at Grassy Point. When a sec-tion was completed, the dry dock was flooded to allow tugs to haul them down the river in a treacherous five-hour journey. The first caisson, also referred to as a box, was finished on October 12, 1953.

The towing of the fabricated sections of the bridge resembled, according to one participant, a Rose Bowl parade with ample noise and even a royal float. Barges bearing falsework had to be towed out at the high water mark and arrive at the bridge site as the tide was ebbing. At "Span Landing," the site of the bridge construction downriver, the tides were used as "a new trick in the bridgeman's bag of tricks." This operation required skill, patience, moderate winds, and calm waters. As the barges approached, the fenders were opened on one side to receive

THE TAPPAN ZEE BRIDGE AND THE FORGING OF THE ROCKLAND SUBURB

AMERICAN BRIDGE DIVISION, U. S. STEEL CORP.
PROGRESS PICTURE
General view looking
Northwest at Bents 176 and 178
TAPPAN ZEE BRIDGE
DATE-Sept. 2,1955
Photographer-L.F. Stockmeyer, Nyack, N. Y.

Photograph showing falsework and the cantilevered section of the bridge *HSRC Collection*

Falsework in place, construction of cantilevered section *HSRC Collection*

Falsework in place, before beginning work on the cantilevered section *HSRC Collection*

Cantilevered section almost completed *HSRC Collection*

Raising a beam into the cantilevered section of the bridge *HSRC Collection*

The Tappan Zee Bridge, almost completed *HSRC Collection*

Aerial photograph, looking east *HSRC Collection*

the caisson. Once in place, each caisson was filled with water and sunk, eventually resting on five layers of sand and gravel 42 feet below. These 40-foot-high buoyant caissons varied in size, with the largest weighing 25,000 tons. As the superstructure added weight, water was pumped out of them to achieve proper buoyancy.

As the driver continues east past the first two towers or piers, moving on to the cantilever arm and the suspended span, he or she is at the highest point on the bridge—138 feet above water. The falsework was an imposing structure as it made its way downriver, measuring 517 feet long, 93 feet wide, and 168 feet high. Once in place, it served as the base of operation for the main span.

The roadway begins its slow descent toward Tarrytown and the driver passes over the east deck truss, the road veering again southward, giving the bridge its graceful S shape. The east deck trestle runs 2,600 feet and is supported by circular cofferdams. The driver reaches Westchester on the rock escarpment in the village of Tarrytown.

One of the constant refrains of the opponents of the Hudson River crossing was the danger imposed by the winter ice flows. How would any structure resist this force of nature, whose power Rocklanders fully understood, given their long experience with the Hudson's ice bridge? Ice was sure to accumulate at the base of the bridge and do damage. Engineers were not unmindful of this concern and placed triangular-shaped upstream ice breakers with steel-sheeted piles to protect the caissons from ebb-tide flows. Seven cofferdams are protected in the deep channel on the eastern side, and timber piles with steel rails defend the western side.

Bridges are made for illumination. The skeletal structure of the Tappan Zee Bridge, almost invisible at night, is electrically outlined by a tracery of lights that is playfully reflected in the river below. This nighttime light show gives the bridge

View from the east side of the Hudson River, looking west, with the completed bridge in the background *HSRC Collection*

a romantic luster in contrast to its functional and businesslike appearance in daylight. The 258 mercury lamps that illuminate the roadway are powered by two different companies and are turned on and off by a special light-sensitive "astronomical" switch.

The ice breakers are protected by 26 navigation lights, with two green lights marking the channel midpoint at the center of the span. The illuminated Tappan Zee is one of the favorite subjects of artists and photographers, who see in these images examples of the technological sublime.

On December 15, 1955, the first automobile crossed the Tappan Zee Bridge. On December 18, the first car crashed on the bridge.

Many people conjectured but few fully anticipated the enormous changes the Tappan Zee Bridge would bring to the region. Former Governor Dewey sent a telegram to the opening-day ceremonies in 1955 saying, "This bridge alone is a symbolic span over which Westchester and Rockland counties will move, virtually overnight, 20 years into the future."

Looking west over the bridge *HSRC Collection*

View from Tarrytown, with the completed bridge in the background *HSRC Collection*

Advertisement for the National Bank of Haverstraw and Trust Company in "Hands Across the Hudson," a December 14, 1955 supplement to *The Journal News HSRC Collection.*
Reprinted with permission: The Journal News/Gannett Co. Inc.

ROCKLAND AS SUBURB

Over the next twenty years Rockland County was radically transformed into New York's newest suburb or, as some said, the city's sixth borough. Although the principal catalyst in this rapid expansion was the Tappan Zee Bridge, events in Rockland were part of a larger national pattern.

The 38.25-mile-long Palisades Interstate Parkway was built between 1947 and 1958, and fully opened to traffic on August 28, 1958. The southern terminus is the George Washington Bridge and the northern terminus is in Fort Montgomery, New York, where the parkway connects to U.S. Route 9W and the Bear Mountain Bridge. It serves as a feeder road to Rockland and a connecter to the thruway. When paired with the Tappan Zee Bridge, it was part of a critical nexus of highway conjunctions that provided modern, speedy automobile access to the county.

The phrase "build it and they will come," from Ray Kinsella's *Field of Dreams*, is fully validated in Rockland's postwar experience. In the four-year period immediately after the completion of the bridge, from 1956 to 1960, the county's population increased by 20.2 percent; from 1960 to 1963 by 18.4 percent; and from 1963 to 1966 by 18.9 percent. The unprecedented scale of this growth—roughly 50 percent in a decade—required Rockland to remake itself on the run.[148] Only the tight mortgage market of 1967–68 slowed the growth rate and allowed the county to catch its breath. But the rate of growth does not in itself tell the full story.

The great Rockland suburban migration was dominated by young families. The most radical increase occurred in the 5–19 age group, which by 1969 accounted for 33 percent of the population, a sharp jump from the 21 percent figure for 1950. When this figure is linked to the growth of the 35–44 cohort, we can document the influx of the young parents. The median age declined from 33 in 1957 to 27 in 1969. These numbers show that the bridge and the county were appealing to new families pursuing the postwar dream of the single-family home. The implications for the infrastructure of Rockland's towns and villages are both obvious and profound.

The first need was for homes. The Federal Housing Administration (FHA) was designed to allow lower down payments, create longer-term mortgages, and reduce monthly costs. The great majority of its loans went to home buyers in the suburbs. Indeed, home ownership increased from 44 percent in 1934 to 63 percent in 1972.[149] Rockland's building boom, which lasted until the late 1960s, was part of this national pattern.

In the fifteen-year period from 1955 to 1969 (excluding 1964–65) new housing construction averaged 2,114 units a year with peaks of 2,600 to 2,800 new units

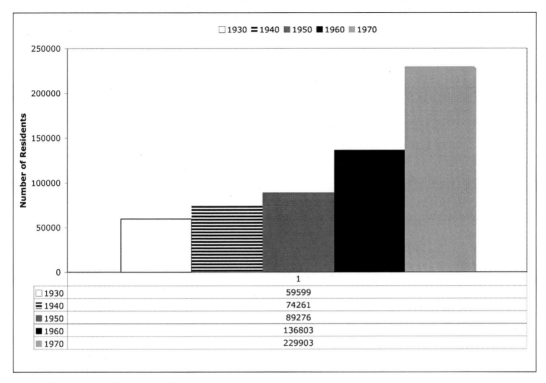

	1
□ 1930	59599
☰ 1940	74261
▦ 1950	89276
■ 1960	136803
▨ 1970	229903

Rockland County Population Growth, 1930–1970 *HSRC*

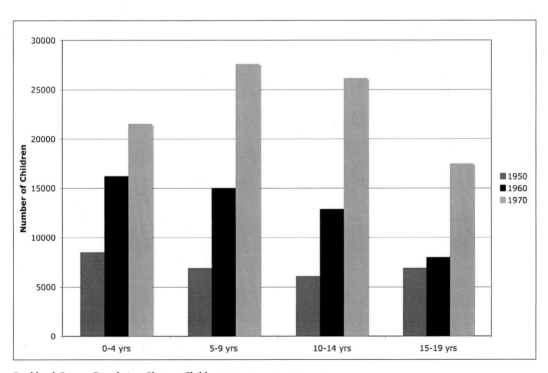

Rockland County Population Change, Children 0–19 years, 1950–1970 *HSRC*

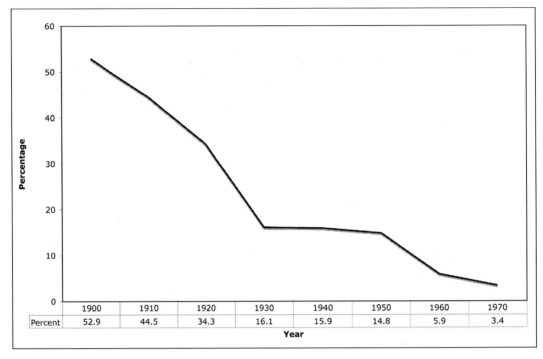

Year	1900	1910	1920	1930	1940	1950	1960	1970
Percent	52.9	44.5	34.3	16.1	15.9	14.8	5.9	3.4

Percentage of Land Farmed, 1900–1970 *HSRC*

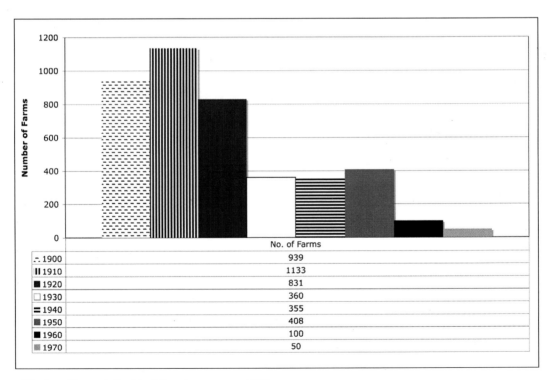

	No. of Farms
∴ 1900	939
‖ 1910	1133
■ 1920	831
☐ 1930	360
≡ 1940	355
▦ 1950	408
■ 1960	100
▨ 1970	50

Number of Farms in Rockland County, 1900–1970 *HSRC*

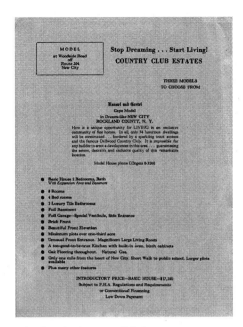

THE JEFFERSON

Sales flyer for Country Club Estates,
New City, NY *HSRC Collection*

Sales flyer for ranch home. Offered for sale by Exurban Realty,
circa 1970. *HSRC Collection*

in 1962 and 1963. Most of the new home construction centered in the unincorporated areas of the five towns—Clarkstown, Orangetown, Haverstraw, Ramapo, and Stony Point. Clarkstown and Ramapo, with the greatest amount of buildable and vacant land, experienced the fastest growth rate, averaging more than 700 new units from 1958 to 1963.[150] By 1969, in all five towns, two of every three residents lived in unincorporated areas—generally in newly built single-family-home subdivisions.[151] The high concentration of new construction would magnify its impact and eventually compel some reaction.

The villages had faster growth rates than the towns between 1966 and 1969 but accounted for only 28 percent of the county's population. Spring Valley and Suffern showed significant gains, while apartment house construction in Nyack and Piermont inflated their numbers. In villages, less buildable land and higher density effectively limited growth. As the suburban juggernaut rolled over Rockland, its vast parkland, one third of the county's land mass, served as a buffer against development, further limiting the amount of available land. These statistics suggest the ways the thruway and the connecting roads determined the pattern of development.

Advertisement for James Stone in "Hands Across the Hudson," a December 14, 1955 supplement to *The Journal-News* HSRC Collection. *Reprinted with permission:* The Journal News/*Gannett Co. Inc.*

Advertisement for apartments at Berkeley Square, Suffern, NY, circa 1970 *HSRC Collection*

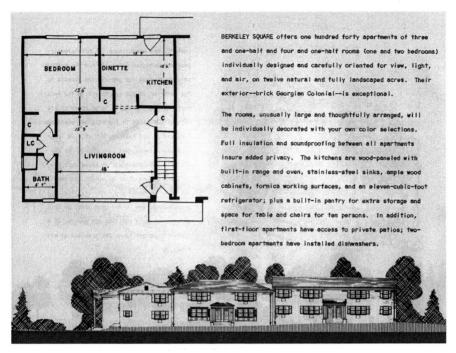

BERKELEY SQUARE offers one hundred forty apartments of three and one-half and four and one-half rooms (one and two bedrooms) individually designed and carefully oriented for view, light, and air, on twelve natural and fully landscaped acres. Their exterior--brick Georgian Colonial--is exceptional.

The rooms, unusually large and thoughtfully arranged, will be individually decorated with your own color selections. Full insulation and soundproofing between all apartments insure added privacy. The kitchens are wood-paneled with built-in range and oven, stainless-steel sinks, ample wood cabinets, formica working surfaces, and an eleven-cubic-foot refrigerator; plus a built-in pantry for extra storage and space for table and chairs for ten persons. In addition, first-floor apartments have access to private patios; two-bedroom apartments have installed dishwashers.

Floor plan for apartment at Berkeley Square, Suffern, NY, circa 1969 *HSRC Collection*

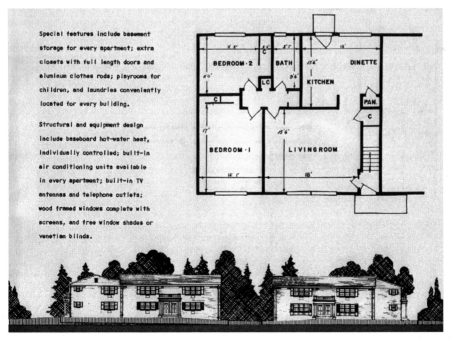

Special features include basement storage for every apartment; extra closets with full length doors and aluminum clothes rods; playrooms for children, and laundries conveniently located for every building.

Structural and equipment design include baseboard hot-water heat, individually controlled; built-in air conditioning units available in every apartment; built-in TV antennas and telephone outlets; wood framed windows complete with screens, and free window shades or venetian blinds.

Floor plan for apartment at Berkeley Square, Suffern, NY, circa 1970 *HSRC Collection*

The keystone of this process of suburbanization was the single-family home, which came to define success and security in the postwar American dream. Such houses constituted the majority of new dwellings, on lots varying in size from a seventh to a quarter acre. They were relatively uniform in design, ranch and Cape Cod styles being the favorites, and constructed in clusters or developments frequently named to promise an eventual community. They were bought on time, an arrangement supported by FHA/Veterans Administration mortgages and encouraged by the real estate and banking industry.

In September 1959 Patricia Sidoti, an apartment dweller in Cliffside Park, New Jersey, noticed a real estate advertisement proclaiming, "Welcome to the Sixth Borough," Orangeburg, New York. The house in the ad was described as a colonial model, the catchphrase for all the revival styles. But the cost of $18,900 seemed out of reach, especially compared to the $10,000 price tag of the homes from the early 1950s immediately after the bridge was completed in 1955. This would be the family's first home. Patricia and her husband drove north on the Palisades Interstate Parkway and in 15 minutes arrived at Exit 6 in Rockland County. A tour of the model won them over. Excitement was tempered by the $20,500 final price tag, but reassurance from her mother and the Realtor about the financing closed the deal. The move was traumatic but the adjustment was quick.[152]

Pat Sidoti stayed in that original first house for forty years and chronicled the changes in her neighborhood: "We were growing at such speed that even we, as people moving from a congested area to the country, were beginning to feel crowded in with too much building going on." She listed the Betsy Ross Estates and the Prel Garden Apartments as examples and excoriated politicians who "chalked it up to progress." Sidoti complained, "We are killing ourselves with our chopping down trees to make room for more houses . . . polluting our waters and air. We feel there should be a limit and let suburbia stay what we had in mind when we all moved to this area."[153]

The Tappan Zee figured more directly in the Michalak family's suburban dream. They crossed the bridge in the fall of 1958 and visited Sunrise Estates in Nanuet. They selected a $17,000 Cape Cod model, put down $1,300, and went off to get married. Delays in completion of the house forced them to postpone their wedding and move in with relatives. When they finally occupied their new home, the first residents in the development, there was no driveway; nor were there street lights, paths, or landscaping. The first night was scary; it was pitch black and they were frightened.[154] The Michalaks felt they were suburban pioneers. The covered wagon was an image often used by mortgage brokers, real estate companies, and automobile dealers as a reassuring metaphor to rationalize the uncertainties and the apprehension faced by many first-time buyers.

The Michalaks' unfinished house is an apt example of the first wave of suburbanization that followed the opening of the bridge. There had been many warnings in the preceding decade about the need to prepare and plan for the inevitable changes. Few politicians or government officials heeded them. Throughout the county, many new home owners complained not only of missed deadlines but also of shoddy construction, inferior materials, and, most critically, missing street lights, sewer hookups, and sidewalks. Who was responsible for these services? In their anger, new residents organized neighborhood civic associations and pressed the builders and the local government for an accounting. The associations helped build community identity and provided the embryonic structure for other local political organizations.

Rockland's suburban home boom was like the proverbial pebble in a pond; it created a ripple of new expectations including public services and private needs. Economic differences, religious services, education, zoning, shopping, culture, and recreation were clearly discernable issues. In fact, a new Rockland was being invented, with few guideposts or plans to lead the way. Much of what happened in the postbridge decade was an improvised response to a radically new set of circumstances.

The economic configuration of Rockland began to mirror changes in the character of the population. The housing boom fueled construction employment. In 1961 there were 1,594 construction jobs; by 1965 the number was 2,969, an increase of 86 percent. In 1954 Rockland had 2,996 retailing jobs in 1,056 firms. An increase of 88 percent brought the number to 5,630 by 1963. Wholesale jobs jumped 31 percent from 1954 to 1963. The all-important manufacturing sector witnessed similar expansion. In 1963 there were 12,772 jobs, a 17 percent gain over 1954, and in 1980 there were 15,700—an increase of 23 percent over that 17-year period.[155]

Many new companies came to Rockland because the bridge gave them access to New York City. In 1957 the New York State Department of Commerce took Sheldon Weinig, President of the Materials Research Company, on a tour of Route 303. Weinig noted the open space, the short twenty-minute trip to Westchester, and the proximity to New York City. Other companies followed, and soon Route 303 was home to many corporate residents.

Business expansion always requires more energy. The power companies struggled to keep up, and in 1958 the two major companies merged to form Orange and Rockland Utilities. They worked feverishly to put in new gas lines and add new electricity customers. By 1960 they had a 30 percent increase in electricity users and a 48 percent increase in gas users. But O & R also faced greater demand from its residential customers in the 1960s; demand for megawatts increased 284 percent by 1970. This extraordinary increase reflected the appliance frenzy that gripped suburbia and the symbiotic relationship between suburbanization and consumerism, which together constituted key elements in the new American way of life. All these additional energy needs required the construction in 1974 of a new power plant at Bowline Point in West Haverstraw.[156]

An educational building boom spread north and west from Orangetown to Clarkstown and Ramapo. The demographic profile of Rockland's new suburban-ites now became crucial. With so many young new families and the drop in the average age, the county would have to deal with an enormous long-term social need. The construction of new schools at every level was urgent and would bur-den town and village finances for a generation. This became one of the surprise costs of the new suburbs and a principal inflator of local taxes. As concern for property values became the watchword in the new suburbs, good schools added value while high taxes were a drag on the line.

In addition to providing schools, local governments had to meet the demand for the amenities of suburban life, including roads, sewers, parks, and street lights. It became so acute that town and villages turned to their zoning codes to defend themselves against this onslaught. Zoning codes had an uneven history in Rockland County. By 1940 only 62 percent of municipalities had them. Clark-stown, an incorporated township, was under strong suburbanizing pressure and rezoned in 1955 in response to the opening of the bridge. It attempted a process of phased growth by concentrating development around existing clusters and re-quiring special permits for building in the protected "development x districts." Clarkstown worked to remove the idea of "building as a right." The restrictions were redrafted in 1967 with modest changes. The objective was to pace develop-ment so that school construction could match population increases.[157]

In 1969 Ramapo took an even more radical approach and, under the direction of Supervisor John McAlevey, treated every new residential development on a special permit basis. Each building application now required a decision from the town board based on a point system. A developer had to have a sufficient number of points based on proximity of the proposed building to sewage, drainage, and recreation. If these elements were lacking, the developer could gain points by pro-viding or financing the services. Thus, unlike the Clarkstown model, which zoned for spatial land use, Ramapo was directing land use over time. The McAlevey model was later abandoned, and Ramapo today has the most zoning problems of any of Rockland's five towns.[158]

Rockland County suburbanization attracted New York City's new emerging middle-class coterie of civil service workers including firemen, policemen, and teachers as well as a varied ethnic mix, including large numbers of Catholics, Orthodox Jews, Haitians, and Latinos.

The Catholic influx, an increase of 44 percent between 1953 and 1957, concentrated in Clarkstown and Orangetown. A new parish, Saint Augustine's in New City, was established, and a new parochial school was added. The growth continued and by 1960 Catholics constituted 34 percent of the county's population.[159] In 1961 Saint Gregory's was founded in Garnerville.

New Square, a Hasidic community in the town of Ramapo with 7,000 people and a cluster of ranch and Cape Cod houses, was founded in 1954. It represents the most orthodox part of the Jewish population, which had had a historic presence and had a resurgence after the completion of the bridge.

Haitians first arrived in the early twentieth century when Dr. Edgar Milford came to Rockland. The Jean-Jacques, Mondesir, and Sorel families arrived after 1948 and provided the original nucleus for the Haitian community, first in central Nyack, then in Spring Valley, and now in Haverstraw. This cohesive, largely Catholic community with stores and cultural centers includes many single-family homes.[160] Their neighbors in Haverstraw are often Dominicans who have followed the Puerto Ricans, who first came to the village in the post–World War II period as agricultural workers. Haverstraw is heavily Latino but has become common ground for both Haitians and Dominicans seeking escape from the urban centers of New York and New Jersey.

The automobile was the catalyst for the consumer revolution that accompanied suburbanization. In Rockland the rapid increase in automobile registration, dealerships, and used car businesses witnessed the central importance of the automobile. Thus it is no surprise that shopping had to be motorized. In 1969 a 750,000-square-foot shopping center, the Nanuet Mall, home to Sears, Bambergers, and a host of other stores, opened, surrounded by a huge parking lot. At the time, 26 additional shopping malls were on the drawing board. The Nanuet Mall was hotly contested, and opponents rightly intuited that this kind of institution would eviscerate the downtown centers of many of the villages and towns that stood as the last vestiges of small-town Rockland.

As the county grew, so did its shopping appetite. In the 1980s talk of an alternative to the Nanuet Mall began. It provoked a storm of controversy and bitter debate. In spite of the inherent problems with the West Nyack site—a former marsh with toxic waste and the African American gravestones in the Mount Moor cemetery—the project went forward, and in 1998 the Palisades Center on Routes 303 and 59 opened. The 3.5 million-square-foot complex of shops, food vendors, and entertainment, an "all-in-one destination," proved attractive to consumers not just from Rockland but also from the wider region. The implicit linking power of the Tappan Zee Bridge was now actualized, and the Palisades Center was now tethered to The Westchester in White Plains to form a shopping corridor, bringing parity to the two counties.

The final phase of suburban development was the corporate campus. In 1967 the Uris Building Corporation proposed a 12-building office complex in the Blue Hill area in Orangetown. Homeowners protested the scale of the project and expressed the fear that Orangeburg Road would become the Long Island Expressway. After much controversy and several lawsuits, the project was reduced from 12 to two buildings, which remained vacant for years.[161] In 1988, when Blue Hill was 90 percent rented, *The New York Times* titled the story, ROCKLAND COMES OF AGE AS A SUBURB.[162]

The completion of the Tappan Zee Bridge not only was an engineering accomplishment but also initiated a great migration of peoples of many races, different classes, various religions, and many points of origin; some came from nearby cities and some from distant places. And they came in search of the postwar American Dream of the single-family home with its promise of community and harmony.

While at times we lament the excesses of sprawl, we need to recognize the aspirations of all who crossed the bridge. This monumental structure bore promises of hope and renewal. The creation of the postwar Rockland suburb was not only part of the great national movement from city to country but also a truly American story, filled with expectations of new beginnings. The building of the bridge was a decisive moment in Rockland's history. And in this new connection, breaching the water boundary, overcoming the obstacles of nature, we find the origins of modern Rockland County. Looking closely at the Tappan Zee Bridge and the changes it precipitated, we glimpse the story of modern America.

BUILDING THE BRIDGE

1952–1955

All photographs courtesy of the New York State Thruway Authority

ont. Hf 53-10 - #7. Embankment (Addendum
T RAMP A, Rt. 303 Interchange By Brewster 4-

Cont. 53-5-#34 - Lkg. N.E. at Excavation
St - S 19+30 - (7-16-54)

Cont. 52-3 #147   Lkg at flooding

NOTES

1. Louise H. Zimm, A. Elwood Corning, Joseph W. Emsley, and Willitt C. Jewell, eds., *Southeastern New York: A History of the Counties of Ulster, Dutchess, Orange, Rockland, and Putnam* (New York: Lewis Historical Publishing Company, 1946), II:624.

2. "Origins of the County Road System" in Linda Zimmermann, *Rockland County Century of History* (New City: Historical Society of Rockland County, 2002), 10–11.

3. Zimm et al., *Southeastern New York*, 710–712.

4. George Hutton, *The Great Hudson River Brick Industry* (Fleischmanns, N.Y.: Purple Mountain Press, 2003), 10, 24.

5. *City and Country*, February 10, 1906. In Zimmermann, *Rockland County Century of History*, 43.

6. Hutton, *The Great Hudson River Brick Industry*, 82.

7. Zimm et al., *Southeastern New York*, 715.

8. Craig H. Long, "The Haverstraw Landslide Disaster," *South of the Mountains* 40, no. 1 (January–March 1996).

9. Long, "The Haverstraw Landslide Disaster."

10. Frank Bertangue Green, *The History of Rockland County* (1886; reprint, New City, N.Y.: Historical Society of Rockland County, 1989), 176.

11. Henry Hall, *The Ice Making Industry in the United States with a Brief Sketch of Its History* (Washington, D.C.: U.S. Department of the Interior, 1880), 24–30.

12. Peter Eisenstadt, *The Encyclopedia of New York State History* (Syracuse: Syracuse University Press, 2005), 406–407.

13. Susan Corica, "Rockland County Fairs," in Zimmermann, *Rockland County Century of History*, 25.

14. Zimmermann, *Rockland County Century of History*, 23.

15. David Cole, *History of Rockland County* (New York: J. B. Beers, 1884), 157. Jeff Schwartz, "Haverstraw's Utopian Experiment," *South of the Mountains* 24, no. 4 (October–December 1980): 5–9.

16. Carl Norstrom, "Haverstraw Community of 1826: A Try at Utopia," *South of the Mountains* 8, no. 3 (July–September 1964); Cole, *History of Rockland County,* 157.

17. Bill Day, "Ehrenfried Pfeiffer, the Threefold Community, and the Birth of Biodynamics in America," *Biodynamics* (Fall 2008).

18. Ralph Borsodi, *Flight from the City: An Experiment in Creative Living on the Land* (New York: Harper & Row, 1933), Chapter 1.

19. John Scott, "Experimental Living," in Zimmermann, *Rockland County Century of History,* 130–132.

20. Borsodi, "Prelude," *Flight from the City.*

21. John Scott, "Experimental Living," in Zimmermann, *Rockland County Century of History,* 132.

22. Eugene Brown, "The Christian Herald Children's Home," *South of the Mountains* 44, no. 2 (Apri–June 2000).

23. Sr. Margaret Harrison, "The Dominican Congregation of Our Lady of the Rosary," in Zimmermann, *Rockland County Century of History,* 12–13.

24. Harold L. Laroff, "The Beginnings of Rockland's Jewish Communities," in Zimmermann, *Rockland County Century of History,* 15.

25. Harold L. Laroff, "The Jewish Community 1910–1919," in Zimmermann, *Rockland County Century of History,* 61.

26. Frances F. Dunwell, *The Hudson River Highlands* (New York: Columbia University Press, 1993), 138–165. Kathyrn W. Burke, *Hudson River Bridges* (Charleston: Arcadia Press, 2007), 25–48.

27. *Piermont: Three Centuries* (Piermont, N.Y.: The Friends of the Piermont Public Library, 1966), 17.

28. *Piermont: Three Centuries,* 18.

29. Craig H. Long, "The Founding of Good Samaritan Hospital: A Big Gift for a Small Village," *South of the Mountains* 36, no. 4 (October–December 1992): 2.

30. Bill Falk, "Ferry Tales of the Hudson," *The Journal-News* (Nyack), September 10, 1978.

31. John Scott, "Gypsies in Rockland County," in Zimmermann, *Rockland County Century of History,* 88–89.

32. Daniel deNoyelles, "Other Bridges Opened Rockland Before the Tappan Zee Did," *South of the Mountains* 31, no. 3 (July–September 1987).

33. Carl Nordstrom, "The Magic of the Automobile," in *Phoenician Tales* (unpublished ms.). Zimmermann, *Rockland County Century of History,* 91.

34. Alan Anderson, "Maxwell Anderson on South Mountain Road," *South of the Mountains* 32, no. 3 (July–September 1988).

35. See Judith Richardson, *Possessions: The History and Uses of Haunting in the Hudson Valley* (Cambridge: Harvard University Press, 2003), 173–203. Provides a full and detailed treatment of Anderson and High Tor, with special emphasis on the use of hauntings and ghosts.

36. Richardson, *Possessions,* 184.

37. Richardson, *Possessions*, 186.

38. Richardson, *Possessions*, 187.

39. Richardson, *Possessions*, 193.

40. *Rockland County Journal,* February 3, 1866. The newspaper accounts of the plans for, public debate about, and construction of the Tappan Zee Bridge draw heavily from Craig H. Long's rich multivolume newspaper archive. I also depended on the "TZB Outline/Timeline" ably organized by Gretchen Weerheim of The Historical Society of Rockland County.

41. *Rockland County Journal,* December 28, 1872 and January 11, 1873.

42. *Nyack Evening Journal,* February 2, 1918.

43. *Nyack Evening Journal,* February 1, 1905.

44. *Nyack Evening Journal,* City & Country section, August 16, 1913.

45. *Nyack Evening Journal,* March 10, 1919.

46. *Nyack Evening Journal,* July 14, 1922.

47. *The New York Times,* August 8, 1925.

48. "Home Comforts in Rockland County," *The New York Times,* December 6, 1925.

49. "Home Comforts in Rockland County," *The New York Times,* December 6, 1925.

50. *The New York Times,* May 28–31, 1929.

51. *The New York Times,* May 28, 1929.

52. *The New York Times,* May 30, 1929.

53. Robert Fishman, "The Regional Plan and the Transformation of the Industrial Metropolis," in David Ware and Oliver Zunz, *The Landscape of Modernity* (Baltimore: Johns Hopkins University Press, 1997), 106–128.

54. *Rockland Leader,* January 16, 1930.

55. *Rockland County Times,* January 18, 1930.

56. *Rockland County Evening Journal,* January 22, 1930.

57. *Rockland County Evening Journal,* February 5, 1930.

58. *Rockland County Evening Journal,* February 7, 1930.

59. *Rockland County Evening Journal,* February 7, 1930.

60. *Rockland County Leader,* February 20, 1930.

61. *Rockland County Evening Journal,* February 25, 1930.

62. *Rockland County Evening Journal,* March 28, 1930.

63. *Rockland County Evening Journal,* September 2, 1930.

64. *Rockland County Evening Journal,* September 23, 1931; *Rockland County Times,* September 24, 1931.

65. *The Journal-News,* August 27, 1936.

66. *The Journal-News,* July 5, 1933.

67. *The Journal-News,* June 6, 1935.

68. *The Journal-News,* June 17, 1935.

69. *The Journal-News,* July 11, 1935.

70. *The Journal-News,* October 26, 1935.

71. *The Journal-News,* September 1, 1936.

72. *Rockland County Leader,* September 10, 1936.

73. *The Journal-News,* September 10, 1936.

74. *The Journal-News,* September 11, 1936.

75. *The Journal-News,* September 12, 1936.

76. *The New York Times,* September 12, 1936.

77. *The New York Times,* September 20, 1936.

78. *The Journal-News,* September 21, 1936.

79. *The Journal-News,* September 22, 1936.

80. Berta and Elmer Hader, "Home Sweet Home: How to Get One," unpublished ms., 1947, copyright 2008 Joy Hoerner Rich. Historical Society of Rockland County.

81. Hader, "Home Sweet Home," 1, 6.

82. Hader, "Home Sweet Home," 10.

83. Hader, "Home Sweet Home," 21–21a.

84. Hader, "Home Sweet Home," 23.

85. Hader, "Home Sweet Home," 38.

86. *The Journal-News,* September 23, 1936.

87. *The Journal-News,* September 25, 1936.

88. *The Journal-News,* September 29, 1936.

89. *The Journal-News,* September 30, 1936.

90. *The Journal-News,* October 2, 1936.

91. *The New York Times,* October 4, 1936.

92. *The Journal-News,* October 8, 1936.

93. *Rockland County Leader,* October 22, 1936.

94. *Rockland County Leader,* October 29, 1936.

95. Scott E. Webber, *Camp Shanks and Shanks Village: A Scrapbook* (New City: Historical Society of Rockland County, 1991), 199.

96. Webber, *Camp Shanks and Shanks Village,* 203–204.

97. Webber, *Camp Shanks and Shanks Village,* 201.

98. Webber, *Camp Shanks and Shanks Village,* 208.

99. Webber, *Camp Shanks and Shanks Village,* 213.

100. Webber, *Camp Shanks and Shanks Village,* 233.

101. Matthew Farish, "Disaster and Decentralization: American Cities and Cold War," *Cultural Geographies* 10 (2003): 125–148.

102. Kristina Zarlengo, "Civilian Threat, the Suburban Citadel, and Atomic Age American Women," *Signs* 24, no. 4 (Summer 1999): 925–930.

103. Farish, "Disaster and Decentralization," 131.

104. Farish, "Disaster and Decentralization," 136–137.

105. Zarlengo "Civilian Threat," 934.

106. Zarlengo "Civilian Threat," 936.

107. Linda Zimmermann, "Missile Air Defense System," in Zimmermann, *Rockland County Century of History,* 189.

108. Martin V. Melosi, "The Automobile Shapes the City," http://www.autolife.umd.umich. edu/Environment/E_Casestudy/E_casestudy9.htm#popsugrue.

109. Edward Dimenberg, "The Will to Motorization: Cinema, Highway, and Modernity," *October* 73 (Summer 1995): 90.

110. Dimenberg, "The Will to Motorization," 100–102.

111. Dimenberg, "The Will to Motorization," 93.

112. Dimenberg, "The Will to Motorization," 104.

113. Dimenberg, "The Will to Motorization," 104.

114. Roland Marchand, "The Designers Go to the Fair II: Norman Bel Geddes, The General Motors 'Futurama,'" *Design Issues* 8, no. 2 (Spring 1992): 23.

115. Marchand, "The Designers Go to the Fair II," 27.

116. Norman Bel Geddes, *Magic Motorways* (New York: Random House, 1940), 276–277. Dimenberg, "The Will to Motorization," 12.

117. Michael R. Fine, *Paving the Way: New York Road Building and the American State, 1880–1956* (Lawrence: University Press of Kansas, 2008), 2–17.

118. Jeffrey R. Brown, Eric A. Morris, and Brian D. Taylor, "Planning for Cars in Cities: Planners, Engineers, and Freeways in the 20th Century," *Journal of the American Planning Association* 75, no. 2 (Spring 2009): 162.

119. Fine, *Paving the Way,* 184.

120. *The New York Times,* February 1, 1945.

121. *The New York Times,* April 25, 1945.

122. *The Journal-News,* December 5, 1945.

123. *The Journal-News* May 22, 1947.

124. *Ramapo Valley Independent,* September 2, 1948.

125. *The Journal-News,* February 14 & 27, 1950.

126. *The Journal-News,* May 1, 1950.

127. *The Journal-News,* April 28, 1950.

128. *The Journal-News,* May 6, 1950.

129. *The Journal-News,* May 10, 1950.

130. *The Journal-News,* May 12, 1950.

131. *The Journal-News,* May 15, 1950.

132. *The Journal-News,* May 19, 1950.

133. *The Journal-News,* May 31, 1950.

134. Fine, *Paving the Way,* 209.

135. *The Journal-News,* January 5, 1951.

136. *The Journal-News,* August 4, 1950.

137. *The Journal-News,* December 11, 1950.

138. *The New York Times,* December 22, 1950.

139. Fine, *Paving the Way,* 146–153.

140. Fine, *Paving the Way,* 225.

141. Fine, *Paving the Way,* 216.

142. Fine, *Paving the Way,* 225.

143. *The Journal-News,* January 31, 1951.

144. *The Journal-News,* October 29, 1953.

145. *New York World-Telegram and Sun,* November 4, 1953.

146. *The New York Times,* August 20, 1953.

147. *US Steel News,* January 1955, 1.

148. Rockland County Planning Board, "Rockland County Population 1969. A Report Based on the Special Census of May 1969," New City, January 1970, 1.

149. Robert A. Beauregard, *When America Became Suburban* (Minneapolis: University of Minnesota Press, 2006), 81.

150. "Town and Village Building Inspectors Records, Residential Building Activity 1950–1980," Rockland County Data Books, Rockland County Planning Board, 1980, 35.

151. Rockland County Planning Board, "Rockland County Population 1969," 3.

152. Mrs. Patricia Sidoti, "Memories of Moving to Rockland," in Zimmermann, *Rockland County Century of History,* 185–186.

153. Sidoti in Zimmermann, *Rockland County Century of History,* 186.

154. Joseph W. Michalak, "Building a Home," in Zimmermann, *Rockland County Century of History,* 186–187.

155. *The Journal-News,* December 15, 1980, D8.

156. *The Journal-News,* December 15, 1980, D8.

157. Joan Margaret Mano, "Zoning, Diffusion, Structure, and Impact: The Case of Southern New York State," Ph.D. diss., Columbia University, 1985, 147–155.

158. Mano, "Zoning, Diffusion," 213–215.

159. Arthur C. Orlando, "The Growth and Development of Roman Catholicism in Rockland County 1953–1963," Unpublished manuscript, May 1965, 14–18.

160. Morton Marks, *Haiti on the Hudson: The Formation of the Haitian Community of Rockland County* (New City, N.Y.: Historical Society of Rockland County, 1993), 7–14.

161. Linda Zimmermann, "The Battle of Blue Hill," in Zimmermann, *Rockland County Century of History,* 237–238.

162. *The New York Times,* September 11, 1988.

ORAL HISTORY PARTICIPANTS

INTERVIEWEES

Rev. Dr. Gordon Anderson
Fulton Oursler Jr.
Richard J. Blauvelt Sr.
Dorothy Buonocore
Don Bracken
John Bristow
Eugene Brown
Harrison Bush
Rita Callan
James and Patricia Cropsey
Mary Crowley
Rita Crowley
Reta Davidson
Niles M. Davies Jr.
Rita DeCarlo
Kathleen DeGroat
Ann DeMeo
Michael DeMeo
Richard and Evelyn DeFreese
Jean Gardner
Jack Geist
Robert Goldberg
Arthur H. Gunther III
Thomas Hackett
Edward C. Hampson
Dennis Hardy
Anna Hickey
William F. Kinslow
Harold Lindland
Richard May
Charles Mouquin
John Munkittrick
Katherine Ogden
Irma Ohmeis
Walter Orland
Mildred Oslica
Frances Pellegrini
Winston C. Perry Jr.

Robert Samuels
Jerome Sandock
Lee Sneden
June Starke
Lauri Steadwall
Jack Stockmeyer
C. Scott Vanderhoef
Gardiner Watts
Jean Jenkins Winter
Dorothy Wonoker
Carl Wright

HISTORIANS

Dr. Travis E. Jackson,
  Oral History Project Coordinator
Robert Goldberg
Jessica Kuhnen
PJ Mouquin
Veronica DeMeo Boesch
Leontine Temsky
Grace Mitchell
Brian Jennings
Alexis Starke

TRANSCRIPTION

Andrew Meier
Gretchen Weerheim
Melissa Sheinman

TAPPAN ZEE STORIES CD

Erin L. Martin
Dr. Travis E. Jackson
David Simons
Carol L. Clarke